# Bring Your "A" Game

# Bring Your "A" Game

## A YOUNG ATHLETE'S GUIDE
## TO MENTAL TOUGHNESS

Jennifer L. Etnier, Ph.D.

Illustrations by Dominy Alderman

THE UNIVERSITY OF NORTH CAROLINA PRESS
CHAPEL HILL

Designed and set by
Kimberly Bryant
in The Serif and The Sans
Manufactured in the
United States of America

The paper in this book meets the guidelines for permanence and durability of the Committee on Production Guidelines for Book Longevity of the Council on Library Resources.

The University of North Carolina Press has been a member of the Green Press Initiative since 2003.

Library of Congress Cataloging-in-Publication Data
Etnier, Jennifer L.
Bring your "A" game : a young athlete's guide to mental toughness / by Jennifer L. Etnier.
    p. cm.
ISBN 978-0-8078-3347-6 (cloth : alk. paper)—
ISBN 978-0-8078-5990-2 (pbk. : alk. paper)
1. Sports—Psychological aspects. 2. Athletes—Training of. 3. Athletes—Psychology. I. Title.
GV706.4.E79 2009
796.001'9—dc22        2009019730

cloth    13 12 11 10 09  5 4 3 2 1
paper    13 12 11 10 09  5 4 3 2 1

FOR PAYTON, JAMES, AND MAX,

*who are helping me to become more patient, loving,*
*and wise. I look forward to helping you become whoever*
*it is that you want to be.*

# Contents

1 · · · Introduction  1

2 · · · What Does It Take to Perform at a High Level in Sport?  5

3 · · · Physical Characteristics  9

4 · · · Technical Skills and Tactical Abilities  23

5 · · · Selecting a Coach and Team  36

6 · · · Mental Toughness  46

7 · · · Goal Setting  51

8 · · · Outcome Goals versus Process Goals  70

9 · · · Attributions  83

10 · · · Self-Talk  94

11 · · · Controlling the Controllables  102

12 · · · Energy Management  109

13 · · · Pre-Performance Routines  125

14 · · · Imagery  135

15 · · · Burnout  145

16 · · · Confidence Building and Maintenance  157

17 · · · Sacrifices, Balance, and Dealing with Disappointments and Adversity  165

18 · · · Dealing with Parents  177

19 · · · Conclusion  187

Acknowledgments  190

Note to Coaches  191

Note to Parents  193

Index  195

# Bring Your "A" Game

# Introduction

Are you a young athlete who wants to perform well in your sport? Do you want to learn mental skills to help you deal with pressure? Do you have dreams of playing at the highest level? Are you interested in getting the most out of yourself? Then this book is exactly right for you! I have designed it for any young person who is trying to be successful in any area of performance. It is specifically written for athletes, but it will also be beneficial to actors, spelling bee contestants, violinists, debaters, and dancers.

I was trained in exercise and sport science, and for the last fifteen years I have been conducting research, working with college athletes, and giving performance enhancement presentations to parents, coaches, and athletes. During this time I have realized that young athletes could benefit greatly from knowledge in the field of sport psychology, yet they are not being provided with this information in any kind of systematic fashion.

I know that young athletes are not getting this important sport psychology information because I see their behaviors at the fields, gyms, and courts. I see young athletes getting frustrated with their play and becoming so upset that they cannot perform. Is this you? I see teams of young athletes going into competition unprepared and losing to teams of lesser skill. Is this your team? And I see young athletes losing so much confidence in their ability and interest in their sport that they consider dropping out of their sport completely. Does this describe your experience? Also, I frequently meet adult athletes who tell me that they have never been exposed to the valuable mental skills that sport psychology offers—skills that they could have been using for years to enhance their performance. Often adult athletes tell me that they have yearned for this

Do you have dreams of achieving a high level of success in some area of performance?

kind of information and that they have had to seek it out themselves as they tried to master their mental skills. The thirst for knowledge apparent in these adult athletes and the stories they tell of their challenges as young athletes make it clear to me that sport psychology skills need to be provided to young athletes.

Not only do I believe that young athletes could benefit substantially from this sport psychology knowledge, but I think it is very likely that a young athlete will benefit even more from sport psychology techniques than will an adult athlete. Thus, the purpose of this book is to provide young athletes with an introduction to the mental skills they will need if they are to reach their potential in sport. Most sport psychology books that have been published are targeted toward older athletes; this book is written at a level that should be appropriate for junior high and high school students. That being said, adult athletes who have not had exposure to sport psychology techniques will also find this book helpful, and younger children who receive some help with the vocabulary could also benefit from this book. The concepts and skills introduced here can be used from childhood to adulthood; however, this book incorporates chapters that are specifically targeted toward young athletes and also includes some comments regarding developmentally appropriate activities for adolescents. I hope that the mental skills presented here will help young performers to harness their energies, focus their efforts, deal with pressure, and maximize their potential so that they can reach their goals. By reading this book, practicing the skills described, and committing yourself to the development of mental toughness, you will be making important strides toward accomplishing your goals in sport.

## How to Use This Book

The chapters of this book are organized in a logical fashion; however, they may also be read independently of one another. So feel free to read the chapters in whatever order makes sense for you. If you have a few minutes, pick out any chapter and read through it! Many people need to read something more than once to really grasp the idea, so there's nothing wrong with reading the chapters a couple of times. As you read the information in a particular chapter, you might be referred to other chapters that provide additional related information to help you with a topic. Feel free to skip ahead to those chapters if you're interested in learning more about those ideas at that time. At the end of the mental toughness chapters, you are provided with exercises and worksheets to practice the skills discussed in the chapter. I encourage you to use the worksheets to help you improve your mental skills. After finishing a chapter, you should begin to incorporate its particular mental skill into your practices and competitions, and even into your free-time activities. By adding more and more of these skills to your mental toolbox, you will begin to develop the mental toughness that is necessary for you to reach your potential in your sport.

Although this book is particularly written for young athletes and is targeted toward sport performance, the information and techniques provided are just as useful for adult athletes and are relevant to any type of performance situation. Essentially, if you have a goal of bettering your performance in any activity, you can benefit from reading this book, adopting the mental skills as your own, and increasing your mental toughness.

---

**EXAMPLES** of sport situations that can benefit from mental toughness:
- You have a goal of playing on your high school varsity team.
- You want to improve your ability to perform in pressure situations.
- You want to increase the consistency of your performance.
- You have just been told that you will be starting in a big game.
- You have just been told that you will *not* be starting in a big game.
- You are having difficulty controlling your anger in games.
- You have just had a season-ending injury.
- You are having trouble maintaining your focus during a game.

**EXAMPLES** of non-sport situations that can benefit from mental toughness:
- You are asked to give an oral presentation in front of your classmates.
- You are experiencing test anxiety and cannot seem to perform well on examinations.
- You are trying out for a part in a play.
- You have a job interview.
- You have a piano recital.
- You are having trouble focusing during a dance routine.
- You are competing in a spelling bee.

---

If any of these or an infinite number of other situations requiring a high level of performance apply to you, then the skills described in this book can help. You are taking the first step by reading about these mental skills. The next step is to begin to make these mental skills a daily part of your preparations and competitions. And finally, you must be willing to practice these mental skills on a regular basis so that you adopt them as your own and so that mental toughness becomes one of your character attributes.

# What Does It Take to Perform at a High Level in Sport?

If you are reading this book, then I am guessing that you have dreams of performing at a high level in your sport. Maybe you want to play in high school or for a good club program. Or perhaps you have goals of playing in college or even professionally. Good for you! To dream of reaching a high level of performance is fantastic and represents a necessary first step toward actually attaining such a goal. But what does it take beyond that? Obviously, many young athletes dream of playing at a high level, but only a very few achieve their goals. In fact, if you were to ask a group of eight-year-old hockey players how many of them want to play college and pro hockey, how many hands do you think would go up? My guess is that in many groups, you would see every single hand raised. But in reality, only a very small percentage of athletes play at the upper levels. So what does it take for an athlete to reach the highest echelons of his or her sport? In addition to the dream of playing at a high level, you must also have the necessary physical characteristics, technical skills, and tactical abilities to be successful; you must be willing to put in consistent hard work to achieve your potential; and you must have access to good coaching and to competitive challenges.

Depending on your particular sport, certain physical characteristics are necessary for you to compete at the highest level. Some of these traits are almost completely genetically determined (you get them from your parents), and others are determined largely by the environment in which you grow up and by your training. Sometimes people refer to this as the nature (what you get from your parents) versus nurture (what you get from the environment) distinction. In addition to physical characteristics, you must also be technically skilled (able to perform the skills required for your sport), and you must have a good tactical understanding of your sport (able to understand the strategies relevant to your sport). Technical skills and tactical abilities are developed through diligent practice and training, good coaching, and exposure to competitive challenges.

Now, is that all it takes? A dream of playing at a high level, certain physical characteristics, technical skills, tactical abilities, coaching, and competition? Clearly all of these things contribute to your ability to be successful, but there is one more critical element that must be in place for you to reach your full potential. A necessary final attribute of athletes who play at a high level is mental toughness. "Mental toughness" is an all-encompassing term that refers to an attitude or a psyche developed by practicing a variety of mental skills that will be discussed in this book. These mental skills include setting goals, managing energy, concentrating on positive attributions, creating mental images, and being able to focus on the "controllables." Additionally, mental toughness is characterized by a willingness to make sacrifices in a variety of ways to achieve the highest level of performance possible for you. The notion, then, is that an athlete who is able to play at a high level starts with natural abilities and a dream; but then through hard work, exposure to quality instruction and competition, commitment, and sacrifice, the athlete develops the physical characteristics, technical skills, tactical understanding, and mental toughness that are required for that athlete to actually reach his or her potential.

In this book, I will only briefly talk about physical characteristics, technical skills, and tactical abilities because these are the attributes that you are developing through practice and with the help of your teammates and coaches. I will also briefly discuss considerations to make when selecting a coach and team to play for. Then I will turn to the primary focus of this book, which is the mental skills necessary to reach the highest level of achievement that is possible for you. This is the one aspect of training that is typically not well understood by coaches and that most young athletes are not formally exposed to. Once you have read about these mental skills and understand how and why they are important, then you will need to incorporate them into your training sessions, competitions, and free time and to practice them just as you would practice the techniques and tactics that are important for your sport. If you are committed to success in your sport, then you must make mental skills training a part of your preparations so that mental toughness becomes one of your strengths. As Dan Gable, head wrestling coach for the University of Iowa and winner of nine national championships, said, "Raising your level of performance requires a proper mentality and meaning from within. This gives you the ability and drive to work on the things necessary to go to a higher level."

## KEY POINTS

• Many young athletes have a dream of playing sport at a high level, but only a small percentage of athletes actually reach that goal.

• Beyond the dream, success in sport is determined by physical characteristics, technical skills, tactical abilities, hard work, good coaching, competitive challenges, and mental toughness.

• Your physical characteristics, technical skills, and tactical abilities will be enhanced by the work you put in during practice and training, by your exposure to good coaching, and by playing in highly competitive situations.

• The focus of this book is on the mental skills that contribute to mental toughness. By making a commitment to the development of mental toughness that is equal to your commitment to the development of your physical, technical, and tactical attributes, you will ensure that you have nurtured all four attributes that are important for playing at a high level.

# My Commitment to Do What It Takes

Sometimes it is helpful for people to create a contract with themselves that spells out their commitment to doing whatever is necessary to reach their dreams. Here is your chance to sign such a commitment that is designed to help you on your way to achieving your dreams.

I, _____, am 100% committed to reaching my dream of _____
_____.

I understand that to achieve this dream is going to require the development of mental toughness, hard work, and sacrifice. By signing here, I demonstrate my commitment to doing everything within my power to give me the opportunity to reach my dream.

_____
        Your signature

# Physical Characteristics

As already mentioned, there are certain genetically based physical characteristics that contribute to success in athletics. Traits that you are born with are sometimes referred to as your "natural" or "God-given" abilities and physical characteristics. Obviously, you will benefit from having certain physical characteristics that are favored in your sport. For example, if you want to play basketball, then height will be an advantage. If you want to play soccer, then speed is an advantage. If you want to be a football player, then both size and speed will be to your advantage. But it is important to remember that these particular characteristics are not necessary for success in any of these sports, and it is also important to remember that many of these characteristics are only partly under your control.

Let me give you an example of what I mean when I say that particular characteristics are not necessary for success. Tyrone "Muggsy" Bogues played college basketball for Wake Forest University, won a gold medal playing for the U.S. national team in the 1986 International Basketball Federation World Championship, was the twelfth pick for the National Basketball Association (NBA) draft in 1987, and played for fourteen years in the NBA. Based on your knowledge of basketball, how tall would you guess Muggsy is? At least 6 feet tall, right? That's a good guess, because the average height in the NBA when Muggsy was drafted was approximately 6 feet 5 inches. But Muggsy was only 5 feet 3 inches tall. He was more than a foot shorter than the average player in the league and nearly 2 feet shorter than some of the tallest players in the league (Manute Bol was 7 feet 7 inches, and Patrick Ewing was 7 feet tall). But, Muggsy did not let his small stature hold him back. Instead, he focused on his other attributes—he was extremely quick and was one of the best passers in

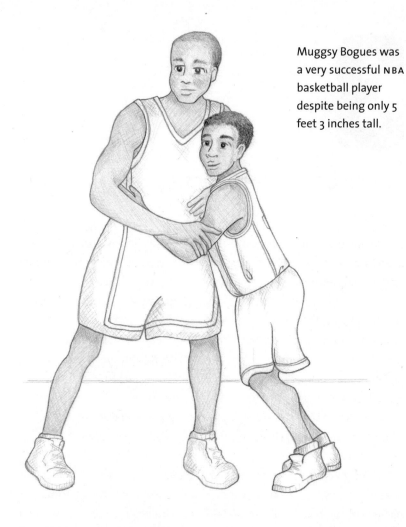

Muggsy Bogues was a very successful NBA basketball player despite being only 5 feet 3 inches tall.

the world—and as a result he had great success in the NBA. So clearly, height is not a necessary attribute for success in basketball, even at the highest level!

In addition to the fact that no particular physical characteristics are absolutely necessary for sport success, it is also important to remember that your physical characteristics are not completely under your control. In other words, no matter how badly Muggsy wanted to be taller, beyond eating a healthy diet, getting enough rest, and participating in regular physical activity as a child, there was nothing that he could do to dramatically change his height. In contrast, your mental toughness, technical skills, and tactical abilities are completely under your control and, combined with your physical characteristics, will ultimately determine your success in sport.

So the key for you as a young athlete is to focus on the controllable aspects of your physical characteristics, your technical and tactical development, and your mental toughness so that you perform at your highest possible level and maximize your likelihood of reaching your dreams. At the same time, you should not worry about things that are not in your control. This will be a recurring theme in this book (see Chapter 11), and I will expand on it here with respect to your physical characteristics.

## Uncontrollable Physical Characteristics

### Height

Allow me to continue discussing the issue of height for just a bit. Sometimes parents ask me whether or not their child should continue in a sport for which he or she does not seem to be physically suited with respect to height. Clearly, there are advantages to being taller in certain sports (e.g., basketball, volleyball, tennis, and fencing) and in certain positions within sport (e.g., baseball pitcher, football quarterback, and basketball center), and there are advantages to being shorter in certain sports (e.g., horse racing, gymnastics, and figure skating) and in certain positions within sport (e.g., football running back). If you are seriously concerned about how your height might affect your chances in a particular sport, then I suspect that your height might not be particularly suited for the sport of your choice. If this is true, then this concern should definitely be given some consideration, but it is not something that you should allow to stop you from pursuing your dream. Let me explain why.

First, as I've already described to some extent, height alone is simply not a very good predictor of success in sport. As previously mentioned, being tall (or short) is not necessary for success in any sport. Athletes with a wide range of heights have been successful in sports for which their height would seem to be a limitation. In addition to Muggsy Bogues (5 feet 3 inches), Jerome "Spud" Webb (5 feet 5 inches) provides another example of a short basketball player who was successful in the NBA. On the flip side, Svetlana Khorkina, one of the stars of the Russian gymnastics team in the 2000 Olympics, is 5 feet 5 inches and looked like a giant among the other female gymnasts, most of whom were less than 5 feet tall. Thus, there are athletes in all sports who are either taller or shorter than is typical for that sport but who have reached the highest level of play possible. Importantly, the examples I've just provided are for sports where height is a much larger contributor to success than it is in other sports. There are many sports, such as soccer, lacrosse, field hockey, track and field, cross country, cycling, and mountain biking, where height does not contribute much to your chances of being successful. In fact, even in beach volleyball, where you'd think height would be critical, Misty May-Treanor (gold medalist in the 2004 and 2008 Olympics) said, "It takes a lot of hard work and dedication just like any pro sport. Especially for beach volleyball you don't have to be tall or as fast as other sports. You just have to have the skills." Thus, although you might be concerned that your height isn't ideal for your sport, it is critical that you remember that height is not the only determinant of success in sport. If your other attributes are strong enough, your height will not stop you from being successful.

The second thing to keep in mind is that it is very difficult to predict what a young person's final adult height will be. There is a difference between your biological maturity (how "grown up" your body is) and your chronological age (how old you are). You may be relatively big or small at a certain age, but this is not necessarily an indication of what your relative size will be when you become an adult. That is, you may have experienced a growth spurt early or late relative to your classmates, and so your current height might be a poor indication of how tall you will be when you are a little older and more mature physically. That being said, if you are short (or tall) for your age and if your parents are also short (or tall) relative to population averages, then it is not likely that you will be a tall (or short) adult. If you are wondering what your final adult height might be, there are formulas that allow you to predict your height based on your parents' heights. Once you see the examples, you will notice that these formulas are not very satisfying because they are imprecise and only provide an estimate with an 8-inch range. However, this is the best there is in terms of predicting height, and you will just have to wait until you reach your adult height before you can be sure how tall you will be!

*Formula for boys:*

[(Mother's height in inches + Father's height in inches) ÷ 2] + 2.5" =
   your predicted adult height ± 4".

*Example for boys:*

If your mother is 5'4" (64") and your father is 6'1" (73"), when you put
   these numbers into the formula, you will get your predicted height:
   [(64" + 73") ÷ 2] + 2.5" = 71" → range = 67" to 75".

This means that based on your parents' heights, you are likely to be
   between 5'7" and 6'3" tall.

*Formula for girls:*

[(Mother's height in inches + Father's height in inches) ÷ 2] - 2.5" =
   your predicted adult height ± 4".

*Example for girls:*

If your mother is 5'4" (64") and your father is 6'1" (73"), when you put
   these numbers into the formula, you will get your predicted height:
   [(64" + 73") ÷ 2] - 2.5" = 66" → range = 62" to 70".

This means that based on your parents' heights, you are likely to be
   between 5'2" and 5'10" tall.

The third thing to keep in mind is that your height is not something that you can exert much control over. You probably noticed that I said that you cannot exert "much" control over height. I say "much" because there is evidence that prior to puberty, adequate nutrition, participation in moderate exercise, and a sufficient quantity and quality of sleep are necessary to ensure that you grow to your genetically determined height. Thus, to ensure that you reach the height that you are genetically capable of attaining, it is important to have a good diet, exercise moderately, and get enough rest. As you might guess, the opposite situation can have a negative effect on growth. When children do not have adequate nutrition, participate in too much physical activity, or are exposed to a great deal of stress, their growth is impeded. They also suffer other negative repercussions in terms of health. Thus, although height can be "stunted" through these negative influences, it is not healthy for

Your height relative to your classmates' might change dramatically from year to year depending on your growth patterns.

a person to experience this "artificial" stunting of growth. If your physical health is not good because of things such as malnutrition, excess exercise, or stress, how can you possibly expect to perform at a high level and to be successful facing the physical demands of athletics? Thus, height is a good example of a physical characteristic that you cannot exert much control over and that you cannot safely manipulate.

So if you wonder if you should continue in a sport for which you believe that your adult height is going to put you at a disadvantage, you can see that there is not really a cut-and-dried answer. Your height will not determine your ability to be successful in sport, you are not likely to be able to accurately predict your adult height, and you cannot significantly (and safely) change your height. Let me speak one more time about the fact that we cannot predict your likelihood of success in sport from your height. Think about this. If we could simply predict success from height at a particular age, the nature of sport as we know it would change because the national governing bodies for the various sports would design programs to select children who fit the size criteria for success in a particular sport and would train them exclusively. Alternatively, those who did not fit the size criteria for success would be discouraged from high levels of competition. Clearly, this does not happen, because height is not a good predictor of success in sport. So with regard to height and sport, height is not a key determinant of sport success, and given that your height is not in your control, I urge you not to worry about your height but instead to focus on those physical characteristics you can control.

### Weight

On a related note, many people seem to believe that a person's weight is something that is completely under his or her control. This is true only at a very minimal level. That is, although all of us can control our weight within a relatively small range, most of us are not able to dramatically change our weight without relying on techniques that can have dramatic and lasting negative health effects (see sidebar 3.1 for a discussion of the negative effects of dramatic methods of weight control). Thus, weight is a physical characteristic that is largely outside your control and, as such, is not a physical characteristic that you should be focused on changing dramatically.

## Controllable Physical Characteristics

Okay, so what about the physical characteristics that you can control? Well, the amount of control that you have over some of these physical factors may still be relatively small. For example, speed and quickness are largely genetically based, so you cannot completely control them through your behaviors. In addition, the amount of time that you devote to fitness training should be based on your level of physical maturity. Physical maturity occurs following puberty, the series of changes in your body that marks your maturation into an adult. In girls, puberty typically begins around age 9, and physical maturity is reached

## 3.1 Negative Effects of Dramatic Weight Control

Many people seem to believe that weight is something that is completely under an individual's control and do not realize that attempts to dramatically change your weight (either to increase or to decrease it) can result in some serious negative consequences. For example, in National Collegiate Athletic Association (NCAA) wrestling prior to 1998, it was common practice for wrestlers to attempt to lose almost 10% of their body weight in a few days to make a certain weight class prior to a competition. At that time, the weigh-in for wrestling in a particular class took place 24 hours before the match, and so the wrestlers could then use that 24-hour period to rehydrate and reenergize to be ready for the match. The weight loss was accomplished over a short period of time by not eating, by losing water weight (through sweating and not replenishing), and by vomiting. This type of disordered eating had dramatic health effects and even resulted in the death of several wrestlers. Thus, there is clear evidence that dramatic efforts to lose weight can result in the worst kind of tragedy. As a result of these serious health implications, most governing bodies for sports in which weigh-ins are required have modified their rules to try to discourage short-term weight loss prior to a competition.

However, longer-term weight restrictions for athletes remain problematic in many sports. This is typically most troubling in sports that reward people for being thin (e.g., gymnastics, figure skating, dancing, cheerleading, and track and cross-country). In these sports, many athletes have practiced disordered eating to the extent that they risk becoming clinically diagnosed with eating disorders. When an athlete is dramatically below his or her healthy weight (15%) for an extended period of time, the negative health consequences are very serious, and that athlete needs to seek professional help. Importantly, evidence clearly shows that athletes who are underweight are not able to perform at their potential. In other words, although their small size might allow them to fit the aesthetic image of a competitor in their sport, they will not be able to perform physically at a level that will contribute to the likelihood of success.

A related issue involves athletes who try to increase their size through the use of drugs. Athletes in sports such as football and weight lifting may be tempted to use illegal drugs such as steroids to try to increase their size and strength. However, it is critical for you to know that although steroids will increase muscle size and body size, there is not clear evidence that such increases contribute to improved athletic ability or strength. I know that if you ask any individual who has taken steroids whether these drugs contribute to strength gain, that athlete will tell you that they do. And, in fact, he or she will likely experience a gain in strength; however, athletes who are taking steroids also simultaneously increase their physical training, so it is not possible to fully distinguish the cause of the strength gain (is it due to the steroids or the increased training?). In addition, evidence shows some short-term negative effects that have implications for your goals in sport. For example, adolescents who take steroids experience a premature halt to their growth, which clearly relates to our previous discussion of how height contributes to success in certain sports. Steroid use also causes weight gain that is detrimental to performance in sports like swimming and track and field. The many serious long-term health effects also have implications for your ability to have a career in sport; these include connective tissue injuries, high blood pressure, anxiety attacks, paranoia, fits of rage, and heart attack. Clearly, these health implications can lead to a shortened career, not to mention a possibly shortened life. Other negative side effects resulting from steroid use by young men include baldness, development of breasts, and infertility; steroid use by young women results in a deepened voice and the growth of facial hair. To me, these side effects are negative enough that they should be discouraging to young athletes considering this illegal course of action. Lastly, I am sure you can recognize that athletes who are taking illegal drugs and have success are not actually winners. They are simply cheaters. They have broken the rules of the sport, and so their victories are not real and, in fact, will be stripped from them when their illegal drug use is discovered.

Finally, with respect to disordered eating, eating disorders, and the use of illegal drugs, most schools, sport clubs, and sport organizations will prohibit you from competing if they find out that you are performing any of these behaviors. If you are caught, the short-term impact on playing your sport is obvious: you won't be playing. If you are not caught, I still believe that the negative effects on sport performance are real: you will be experiencing the previously mentioned negative side effects, you will be experiencing the added stress of trying to keep hidden your illegal drug use or eating disorder, and you will never know if you could have been successful without these behaviors. The long-term effects should also be obvious: the risk of death from steroid usage, from disordered eating, and from clinical eating disorders is real. You have only to read the following names of a few athletes who died due to these behaviors to understand this risk: baseball players Rob Garibaldi (1988–2002) and Ken Caminiti (1963–2004), gymnast Christy Henrich (1972–1994), professional ballerina Heidi Guenther (1975–97), and college wrestlers Billy Saylor (1978–97), Joseph LaRosa (1975–97), and Jeff Reese (1976–97).

So the message is that weight is a physical characteristic that you have some control over but that you cannot change dramatically without harming yourself. If you are tempted to use illegal drugs or practice unhealthy eating or dieting behaviors, don't give in to the temptation. These practices are *not* likely to help your performance in sport and may result in both short-term and long-term negative consequences. If you are already in the vicious cycle of these negative behaviors, I encourage you to seek professional help by consulting with someone you trust and with whom you feel comfortable discussing this issue.

by around age 15. In boys, puberty typically begins around age 10, and physical maturity is reached around age 16.

## *Prepuberty*

If you have not yet reached physical maturity (in other words, if you are a girl who is younger than 15 or a boy who is younger than 16), then you should *not* be spending a lot of your training time on fitness training, speed training, or heavy weight-lifting exercises. There are three primary reasons for this.

First, before you reach physical maturity, the gains in aerobic fitness, speed, and strength that you see are primarily due to your body maturing and to improvements in neuromuscular coordination; they are not due to the training that you are participating in. That is, the gains in fitness, speed, and strength that you see are not a direct result of the training per se. Rather, they are simply due to practicing the movements required for the training and your development into a young adult.

Second, this is the age when practice really does help you to approach perfection in your performance because during these years you are able to refine your performances so that the techniques of the sport become automatic. In other words, by repeatedly practicing a crossover dribble in basketball, a forehand volley in tennis, an overhand serve in volleyball, or blocking in football, the skill will become automatic. This means that the skill will become second nature to you so that you do not have to concentrate to perform the skill and you can perform it well even in highly stressful situations. For this reason, lifting weights or doing fitness training is not the best use of your time. Given that you should only spend a certain amount of time per day training for your sport (see Chapter 17 on balance), you should make the best use of that time. Therefore, if you have not yet reached physical maturity, it is much more important to devote your practice time to the repetitive performance of your sport skills than to devote time to fitness training.

A third reason to put off these types of fitness training until after puberty is the high risk of burnout from repeated performance of the intense and fatiguing activities necessary to gain strength and fitness. Burnout means that you lose interest in the sport and that you are no longer motivated to devote your energies to the activity (see Chapter 15). Burnout occurs when athletes spend too much time performing repetitive and tiring activities like weight training. While it is beneficial to learn the appropriate techniques to improve aerobic fitness, strength, and speed at any age, if you have not yet reached puberty, then the benefits of more intense training will not be worth the increased risk of burnout. See sidebar 3.2 for a story on burnout.

### Puberty

If you have gone through puberty (for most girls, this will occur around 15 years of age; for most boys, around 16 years), then your body is moving toward physical maturity and you should begin to incorporate fitness, speed, and strength training into your performance enhancement program. In particular, you should seek assistance to design a program that includes aerobic fitness training, speed training, quickness (or agility) training, flexibility work, and strength training. Again, speed and quickness are largely genetically determined, but you should include them in your training program so that you improve on your form and to ensure that you maximize your potential with regard to these factors. In contrast to speed and quickness, aerobic fitness, strength, and flexibility are much more readily changed, and you will benefit greatly from an exercise regimen designed to enhance these characteristics.

As you begin to include fitness training in your program, please be sure to refer to reliable sources of information to learn how to en-

## 3.2 Burnout Experienced by a Women's Collegiate Basketball Player

Elena Delle Donne is a young woman who was predicted to be the next great female college basketball player. She received a scholarship to play basketball at the University of Connecticut (UConn) and was expected to help lead that team to a national championship. However, Elena started taking college classes in the summer and realized that she was not happy. After years of training to be a basketball star, she finally admitted that she wasn't really happy and that she hadn't been happy playing basketball since she was about thirteen years old. She left UConn and went to the University of Delaware, where she started playing volleyball. Elena is an example of a young athlete who has burned out on her sport. The reason for her burnout is likely the fact that she started training seriously as a basketball player when she was six years old. As a teenager, she was getting up early in the morning to run, and then later in the day she would practice and do strength training. "I was overdriving myself because I was so into becoming the best," Elena said. "I always thought someone else was working harder than me, which really made me go nuts with it. It wasn't fun. It was like a job, and it was a job I wasn't getting paid for." Before you have reached physical maturity, really consider putting your emphasis on enjoying playing your sport (and other sports that provide complementary training) and hold off on the physical training until later. This will help you to maintain balance and to enjoy your sport while continuing to develop your athletic skills.

hance your aerobic fitness, strength, flexibility, speed, and quickness. Also, as you begin to incorporate these types of training into your program, please recognize that this training should be done in moderation to minimize the risk of injury, overtraining, and burnout (see Chapter 15). Finally, the best programs maintain the performance of the sport skills as a part of the training programs. For example, if you are a tennis player, your quickness training can come in the form of footwork exercises or volleying activities that emphasize quickness in combination with the skills of the sport. If you are a soccer player, your fitness training can come in the form of one-versus-one activities with a soccer ball that also allow you to work on both your offensive and defensive skills. Whatever sport you play, be creative as you identify ways to incorporate speed and quickness, aerobic fitness, strength, and flexibility training with the skills relevant to your sport.

## KEY POINTS

• Physical characteristics do not, by themselves, determine success in sport.

• You should not expend any mental or physical energy on physical characteristics that are outside your control (e.g., height).

• You should not try to dramatically change your height or your weight because the risks of doing this clearly outweigh any benefits that you might think you could obtain.

• If you have not reached physical maturity, you should focus on skills training rather than on fitness training because at this age, the gains you see in strength, fitness, and speed are related to improvements in coordination that can be developed in sport-related activities.

• If you have reached physical maturity, then you should begin to incorporate fitness training into your program so that you maximize your potential with respect to your aerobic fitness, strength, flexibility, speed, and quickness.

# The Physical Characteristics of Your Sport

1. Identify the physical characteristics that are important in your sport.

2. Circle the physical characteristics that can be changed through training. Draw a line through those that cannot be changed.

3. Identify ways to incorporate improvements to these physical characteristics into your training program.

| *Example* | *Your Sport* |
|---|---|
| Basketball | |

| Important Physical Characteristics | Important Physical Characteristics |
|---|---|
| 1. ~~Height~~ | 1. |
| 2. Upper Body Strength | 2. |
| 3. Lower Body Strength | 3. |
| 4. Core Strength | 4. |
| 5. Speed | 5. |
| 6. Quickness | 6. |
| 7. Jumping Ability | 7. |
| 8. Balance | 8. |
| 9. Endurance (Aerobic Fitness) | 9. |
| 10. ~~Long arms and fingers~~ | 10. |

# Technical Skills and Tactical Abilities

In addition to your physical characteristics, your technical skills and tactical abilities will also determine how successful you are in your sport. First, let me explain what I mean by technical skills and tactical abilities. When I speak of technical skills, I am referring to the skills and movements that are necessary for the performance of your sport. For example, in soccer, important technical skills include dribbling the ball with your feet, controlling the ball out of the air, heading, and shooting. In American football, important technical skills include catching the ball, blocking, and tackling. When I speak of tactical abilities, I am talking about knowledge of the game, comprehension of game strategies, and an ability to "see" the game. For example, in soccer, important tactical abilities include knowledge of the roles of the defenders, comprehension of the importance of switching the point of the attack, and being able to "see" when a teammate is open to receive a pass. In American football, important tactical abilities include recognizing a blitz, identifying a coverage scheme, and knowing which side of the field will have the least defensive pressure.

## Technical Skills

The development of technical skills begins when you learn the basics of the sport, even at a very early age. From the minute you pick up a tennis racket or a baseball bat and start trying to contact the ball, you are working on your technical skills. The refinement of these abilities comes through repeated performance in practice settings. This is why your coaches ask you to perform the same activity over and over and over. Only by repeating certain movements can you learn to perform them smoothly and automatically in competition. As you become more advanced in your sport, clearly the level of skill displayed in your technique will progress. For example, a beginning basketball player will concentrate only on the basic skill of dribbling the basketball, but a more experienced player will begin to focus on changing direction and speed with the ball and on feinting to lose a defender. Regardless of your current level, repetitions of a motor skill are needed to ensure that the skill becomes and stays automatic for you. Repeating a skill until it becomes automatic will help to ensure that you can perform the skill well in competition. As Jan Ebeling, gold medalist in the 2003 Pan American Games for dressage, said, "It is better to go the slow route and address the basics. In the long run, you will actually move along faster, as you won't have to go back and fix things."

## Tactical Abilities

In contrast to technical skill development, which begins at your first exposure to a sport, the development of tactical abilities tends to start only after you've gained a certain degree of mastery over the technical skills. Until you have some basic level of skill in the sport, tactics are not particularly relevant. For example, in tennis, until you can actually hit a serve over the net and into the service court, the development of a tactical plan to play a serve and volley style will not be very useful. In softball, until you are able to bunt the ball, you cannot begin to consider the tactical decision of forcing a squeeze play by bunting so that opponents have to decide whether to force you out at first base or to try to tag out your teammates who are trying to advance a base. Once you have developed your basic technical skills, your tactical abilities will begin to develop as you are repeatedly exposed to gamelike situations. This is why your coaches will often include gamelike situations in your practices. For example, during a basketball scrimmage, your coach might ask one "team" to run a full-court press so that the other "team" can practice making tactical decisions to break the press. Or, in lacrosse, your coach might ask you to pretend that you are down by one goal with three minutes to play so that you can practice making tactical decisions under a high-pressure situation. Good coaches who design meaningful practice sessions, who include scenarios (gamelike situations) in their practices, who provide insightful analyses of competitions, and who encourage you to learn from observation of the game itself will create a positive learning environment that will further facilitate the development of both technical skills and tactical abilities. The coach clearly plays a big role in helping you to perfect your technical skills and develop your tactical abilities, so it is crucial that you get good coaching throughout your development as an athlete (see Chapter 5).

## Hard Work

So beyond getting good coaching, what else do you need to do to ensure that you develop sound technical skills and advanced tactical abilities? The simple answer is "hard work," and the responsibility for doing this is completely your own. Your development as an athlete is up to you. No one else can do this work for you. Are you willing to work hard to improve as an athlete? Are you willing to make the sacrifices necessary to improve your technical and tactical abilities? These are important questions that you need to ask yourself if you really want to improve in your sport. Michael Phelps, who has won the most Olympic gold medals of any athlete in history, described this well when he said, "If you're not on your 'A' game in our workouts every day, you're going to get absolutely smoked."

Many young athletes have enormous potential and are on good teams with great coaches but never develop into the athletes they could be. The key factor in these situations is the athlete; he or she is not working hard to take advantage of natural abilities and of the resources available to him or her. The result is that the athlete's technical skills and tactical abilities do not improve as much as they could. To get the most out of your practices, you must learn to be objectively aware of your abilities, to identify your strengths and weaknesses, and to *work* to improve in all areas (even those that you are already good at). To be the best you can be, you will have to work on your own or with a teammate outside of practice, you might need to hire an outside skills trainer or attend teaching clinics, and you may need to ask your coaches to spend extra time with you. The hard work that you put in during practices, games, and your own training sessions will pay off as you move through the ranks in your sport.

I cannot emphasize enough the importance of realizing that working hard is essential, regardless of how good you are right now. As Jahangir Khan, the greatest squash player in history, said, "Without hard work and discipline it is difficult to be a top professional." Let me give an example of why hard work is equally important for a young athlete. Charlie is thirteen years old and clearly the most skilled player on his hockey team at the start of the season. His coaches and his parents and teammates all tell Charlie that he is the best player on the team. Charlie buys into what everyone is telling him and begins to feel that he is a "superstar" and does not need to work hard in practice to maintain that status. So Charlie continues to perform well in practices and competitions, but he does not work to improve his game. He does not give 100% at practice, and he doesn't do any work on his own outside his formal team practices to try to improve. Meanwhile, the other players on his team who were not as skillful as Charlie at the beginning of the season put a lot of time and effort into their practices and train outside practice to improve their skills. By the end of the season, Charlie has fallen behind his teammates and is no longer even one of the better players on the team. He has essentially wasted an entire season and has not improved at the same pace as his teammates. Charlie allowed his early successes to distract him from working hard and did not take responsibility for his own development. Do not fall into this trap of early success. Regardless of your current skill level, it is crucial that you continue to work hard so that you will continue to improve. Only by continuing to improve will you give yourself the opportunity to reach your potential in your sport.

I'll never forget an example of this point that I saw with adult athletes. The U.S. women's soccer team had just completed a two-hour practice on a hot day in Phoenix, Arizona. The team headed to the locker room for a shower and a cold drink, with a single exception. One lone player stayed out on the field after the two-hour practice: Michelle Aikers, who was at that time considered to be the best female soccer player in the world. Instead of going inside to cool down and relax, Michelle stayed afterward for thirty minutes to practice taking free kicks. She asked the staff members who were still on the field to make a wall (this is a defensive technique used in soccer to make it harder for the person taking the free kick to put the ball in the goal), and she took shot after shot after shot. Does this seem surprising? Why would the best player in the world need to stay for thirty minutes of extra practice when all of the other players had called it a day? Since she was the best player in the world, she should not need to stay to practice longer than the other players. But you've probably figured out that this is not the right interpretation of what I saw. In fact, the opposite is true: Michelle Aikers was the best

Although Michelle Aikers was considered the best soccer player in the world, she practiced taking free kicks over and over after others had already left the field.

player in the world *because* she stayed to practice after the other players had quit for the day! Staying behind for thirty extra minutes was what Michelle chose to do because she wanted to maintain her status as the best player in the world. Michelle Aikers is the perfect example of a great player who wanted to be even better. By putting in additional time and work, Michelle could stay the best player in the world, but the minute that she quit putting in the time and effort, other players would begin to catch her.

## Focus

Another point to be made with respect to technical skills is that improvement results from the constant repetition of correct performance. This is the old saying "Perfect practice makes perfection possible." The challenge for a young athlete is that repetition can also lead to boredom, which can result in a lack of motivation to practice. So you've got to learn how to minimize your chances of getting bored in your practices. If you are working with a good coach, he or she will show you a variety of ways to practice your skills and perform many repetitions so that you perfect your skills. A good coach will also structure the practices to make sure that they are not so repetitive that they become boring. To do this, a good coach will give you lots of repetitions but in changing situations. For instance, maybe you'll hit a forehand volley over and over while the tennis coach tosses you the ball. Then you'll hit a forehand volley over and over while the coach hits you a ball from the service line. Then you'll hit a forehand volley over and over while the coach hits you the ball from the baseline. Then you'll hit a forehand volley during a series of groundstrokes. By slightly changing the situation and increasing the difficulty, the coach gets you to repeat the forehand volley a hundred or even a thousand times but keeps you from getting bored by incorporating variety into the session.

Even though a good coach will try to keep practices enjoyable and beneficial, it is still your responsibility to create your own challenges, stay focused during practice, work toward your personal goals, and maintain high levels of effort. Only through repetition will the performance of a skill become automatic, and you want all of the basic skills of your sport to become automatic. As Ian Thorpe, winner of five Olympic gold medals, said, "I swam the race like I trained to swim it. . . . I just let my body do it. It is a lot easier if you let your body do what it is trained for." Ian's point is that he practiced hard and frequently enough that his body could perform automatically even on the biggest stage in sport—the Olympics. Becoming automatic means that the skill can be performed properly in a wide range of competitive situations, at a variety of energy levels, and across different game situations. Therefore, when focusing on skill development, expect to perform the same skill over and over. But avoid becoming bored by creating variety where possible, by focusing on the task at hand, and by concentrating on improvement of the subtleties of the skill.

## Listen and Learn

You must be able to listen and learn from those around you to continue to develop your skills and your tactical abilities. You must be willing to accept constructive criticism and use that feedback to improve your performance. In other words, when your coach tells you that you are not performing the skill properly, you need to be open to that comment and willing to try to change how you perform the skill. For some people, listening and being willing to change are not easy, but you can bet that the best athletes are open to suggestions and are able to change their behaviors to continue mastering their sport. Ronaldo, a Brazilian soccer player who was a key player in winning two World Cup championships, expressed this clearly when he said, "I'm not a phenomenon, just a twenty-one-year-old footballer who still has a lot to learn." As an aspiring young athlete, recognize that no matter how good you are, you still have more to learn. Practice the skill of listening and be strong enough and confident enough to ask others to judge your performance. Feedback from others is a powerful tool for identifying weaknesses and making modifications in your game so that you will perform better. As John Wooden, head coach for the men's basketball team at the University of California at Los Angeles and winner of ten NCAA championships, said, "Good players can take coaching; great players can take coaching and learn."

## How Much Time and Practice Are We Talking About?

As a final note, I think it is important to make you aware of some research that is relevant to these points regarding the need for practice and hard work. Dr. K. Anders Ericsson is a researcher who has studied the development of expertise in a variety of activities. He has interviewed elite athletes, famous musicians, and master chess players. From these interviews, Dr. Ericsson has discovered that regardless of the particular activity, experts in their fields typically report having participated in approximately 10,000 hours of training to develop their expertise. Now, 10,000 hours of training is a lot! A person who began playing his or her sport at age six and who was an "expert" in the sport at age twenty would have had to put in approximately 2 hours per day every day for those 14 years to accumulate 10,000 hours of practice and to achieve this level of excellence. Although this is just an example, you can see that practicing 3 times per week with your team for 1.5 hours per session is not likely to result in you becoming an "expert" in your sport. So the message is clear. If you want to truly commit to excellence in your sport and if you want to play at the highest level possible, then regardless of the age at which you begin to play your sport, you are going to have to devote yourself to practicing in formal sessions and on your own, and you must work hard so that you get the most out of those practice sessions. There is an old adage that makes this idea clear: "The more you sweat in practice, the less you bleed in battle."

Dr. Ericsson also found that there is a real difference in the nature of the practice sessions that the experts completed as compared with the practice of people who never became experts. The key is that the experts participated in "deliberate practice" and often described being creative in how they incorporated practice into their lives. Deliberate practice means that when they put in these 10,000 hours, those individuals who became experts used those 10,000 hours purposefully: they concentrated on improving particular aspects of their performance, they accepted criticisms of their performance and worked to improve, and they were able to self-evaluate so that they could identify their own shortcomings when not working with a team or coach. Young athletes who grasp this point will benefit from practicing deliberately. Casey Keller was a longtime member of the U.S. national soccer team and one of the first U.S. goalkeepers to play professional soccer at the highest level in England (the English Premier League). Casey credits his success to his long-term focus and work ethic. Casey said, "I succeeded because I had a good work ethic. I wanted to be a professional athlete ever since I can remember." If your goal is to play at a high level, then having a good work ethic, practicing with a purpose, being open to feedback, and learning to evaluate and modify your own performance will be keys to your development.

A second point is that many experts are very creative in how they fit practice into their daily lives. For instance, I think of the basketball player who dribbles a basketball everywhere that he goes. I think of the soccer player who plays a game of "soccer tennis" with a friend. I think of the hockey player hitting a tennis ball against a wall for hours with her hockey stick. I think of a pianist practicing a song by drumming his fingers on a desktop. People who become experts make a commitment to practice, and they practice frequently, deliberately, and creatively.

Now, after making these points, let me also point out that 10,000 hours is what is typical. This exact number of hours of practice is certainly not required to become an expert, nor will it guarantee that a person becomes an expert. I say this because if you did not begin to play your sport when you were six years old, you should not be discouraged. The point here is that no matter what age you are when you commit seriously to improving yourself at your sport, you must recognize that to improve significantly will require a meaningful time commitment and deliberate and creative practice. LeBron James, rookie of the year and NBA all-star, described this well when he said, "Ask me to play. I'll play. Ask me to shoot. I'll shoot. Ask me to pass. I'll pass. Ask me to steal, block out, sacrifice, lead, dominate. ANYTHING. But it's not what you ask of me. It's what I ask of myself."

### KEY POINTS

• Technical skills begin to develop as soon as you start to learn the game. They become automatic through repetition (practice) and become more refined with experience.

• Tactical abilities develop through exposure to gamelike situations. Good coaches create gamelike situations (or scenarios) and ask you to respond.

• To develop your technical skills and tactical abilities, you must make sure that you receive good coaching, learn to identify your strengths and weaknesses, and work hard to improve your game.

• To improve as an athlete, you must be willing to accept constructive criticism and feedback, and you must be able to change your behaviors.

• TAKE RESPONSIBILITY FOR IMPROVING YOUR OWN GAME. Work hard in practice to get the most out of these sessions and commit to training on your own to increase your exposure to the game.

# Identifying Where You Are Now

It is important that you are objectively aware of your abilities so that you can identify your strengths and weaknesses. Once you have identified these, you should focus on improving your strengths and minimizing your weaknesses.

## *Strengths*

List some of your strengths. Identify why each is important and describe steps that you can take to continue to improve in these areas.

| EXAMPLE | CONTRIBUTION | STEPS TO IMPROVE |
|---|---|---|
| Shooting ability with dominant hand/foot | Team can count on me to get a good shot off from that side. | Work on shooting from a variety of situations and against a strong defense. |
| Ball handling skills | Team can count on me to get the ball safely through the defense. | Learn new moves (feints); work on vision of field/court while moving with the ball. |
| Work ethic during practice | Encourages others to also work hard so we all improve. | Continue to work hard; keep up the same intensity during games and my own training. |

| EXAMPLE | CONTRIBUTION | STEPS TO IMPROVE |
| --- | --- | --- |
|  |  |  |
|  |  |  |
|  |  |  |
|  |  |  |
|  |  |  |
|  |  |  |

## Weaknesses

List some of your weaknesses. Explain how these hurt the team or your own performance. Identify how you can improve these areas.

| EXAMPLE | HOW IT HURTS PERFORMANCE | STEPS TO IMPROVE |
|---|---|---|
| Shooting ability with nondominant hand/foot | I cannot get a good shot off from that side. | Need to work more with this side during practices and on my own. |
| Defense | My poor one-versus-one defending means others have to defend for me. | Concentrate on defense in practice. Observe others to learn more about defensive positioning. |
| Focus during competition | I am not 100% focused all of the time and sometimes miss opportunities. | Become aware of when focus is fading. Use mental cues to regain focus. |

| EXAMPLE | HOW IT HURTS PERFORMANCE | STEPS TO IMPROVE |
|---------|--------------------------|------------------|
|         |                          |                  |
|         |                          |                  |
|         |                          |                  |
|         |                          |                  |
|         |                          |                  |
|         |                          |                  |
|         |                          |                  |

# Selecting a Coach and Team

To reach your potential in sport, you need to work with a coach or coaches who provide you with the necessary environment to develop your technical skills and tactical abilities. This brings up two important points. First, even at an early age, you should seek out the best coaching that you can find. Doing this might not be easy, and you should recognize that you might have to make sacrifices to gain access to the best coaching available. For example, I know of a player in North Carolina whose parents drove her two hours roundtrip every Tuesday and Thursday afternoon so that she could practice with the best club team in her region. Clearly, the sacrifice in time and energy was large for both the athlete and her parents. However, she was able to train regularly with a highly competitive team and a talented coach, and ultimately she experienced a dramatic improvement in her technical skills and tactical abilities.

Second, you may have to train and/or compete with more than one coach (or team) to get access to the coaching and competition that you need to improve. For example, if you are playing for your school team, then you will be playing for the coach who was hired to coach at that school. So if you are assigned to a particular school, then you will be playing at the level of competition that the school sports provide. If you are at a school and in an area where the competition and coaching are both good, then you will have opportunities to improve. But if you are at a school or in an area where either the competition or the coaching is not good, then it will be hard for you to reach your full potential. This is a difficult situation. To change schools or school districts might mean that your family would have to move, that you would have the added stress of leaving your old friends and making new ones, and that you might lose a year of eligibility (this is now common practice at the high school level). However, another solution might be to play for another team as well. Many sports in the United States now offer opportunities to compete both inside and outside the school setting. For example, in basketball, volleyball, soccer, baseball, softball, and swimming, club sport programs provide access to alternative coaches and competition. Some sports like ice skating, gymnastics, and fencing are not offered in most schools, which gives you some freedom to choose a coach and/or team.

If you have the opportunity to select a team and coach to play for, then deciding on a good coach will depend on several characteristics of the coach and the team that he or she coaches. The variables you need to consider are many, and it is often not easy to get yourself on the right team; but if your goal is to play at a high level, then this is an important key. To identify the coach and team that will help you to reach your potential, you (or perhaps your parents) will need to gather some information regarding the style and qualifications of the coach and the interactions and attitudes of the team. In selecting a coach and team, you should consider the following questions.

## Does the Coach Know the Sport?

This might seem like a crazy question to ask, but there are many instances where coaches are in place who have never played the game that they are coaching! Although in rare cases, such a coach might have a lot to offer, it is more likely that you will benefit from being coached by someone who has experience with and knowledge about the sport you are playing.

In some sports, coaches are able to get coaching certifications that provide evidence of their knowledge of the game. For example, in soccer, coaches can be certified at levels ranging from G (the lowest) to A (the highest). As the coach moves up the certification ladder, the requirements for certification become increasingly challenging, and so a coach who holds a higher license has demonstrated a higher level of knowledge of the technical and tactical information relevant to soccer. If certifications are possible in your sport, then you should seek out coaches with these types of credentials. If certifications are not available in your sport, you can gain insight into a coach's knowledge by finding out about his or her history with the sport and coaching experiences. In other words, find out if the coach played at a high level (like collegiately or professionally) and find out if the coach has coached teams or players that have had success. Although there are certainly good coaches out there who didn't play at a high level or whose teams have not yet had success, this assessment provides a good starting point for understanding the knowledge, experiences, and coaching skills that the coach has to offer.

## Can the Coach Relay His or Her Knowledge to the Athletes?

This is a second important consideration—can this coach relay his or her knowledge of the game to the players? There are many coaches who were fantastic competitors and who know their sport inside and out, but who are not good teachers. It is important that you gather information to try to determine whether or not the coach is a good teacher. Good teachers make good coaches. Good teachers demonstrate the ability to clearly explain skills and drills, they can critique performance in a positive fashion, they have the respect of their athletes, and they are good role models. To find out if a particular coach is a good teacher, you may want to talk to the athletes who are currently working with him or her to see what they think regarding the coach's teaching ability. Or, if possible, try to observe the coach in a coaching situation to see whether or not he or she can actually *teach*. As a final indication, you can look at the success rate of the coach's athletes in higher levels of competition. For example, how many of the coach's athletes have made their high school teams? Or have played collegiately? Or have made a state or regional select team? Although the success of the athletes is not completely in the coach's control, if a coach has helped athletes reach higher levels of competition, then it is likely the coach is a good teacher and mentor for young athletes.

## Are the Other Team Members Motivated and Skilled?

A third consideration is whether or not the other members of the team are motivated and skilled so that you will be challenged in your practices. This assessment is extremely important. To perform at your highest level, you must have regular exposure to other talented athletes who can challenge you to improve your skills. Although you can get exposure to high-level athletes through your competitions, relying on this approach is not the best way to challenge yourself, for several reasons. First, competitions do not happen very often (maybe once a week?), so you do not get enough opportunities to perform against challenging opponents. Second, within the course of a competition, you will not get the chance to repeat a skill over and over. For example, in practice the coach can set up one-versus-one situations in which you are repeatedly challenged to match your offensive and defensive skills against an experienced opponent. However, in a real game, a one-versus-one situation might only occur a few times, so you will not get many of these opportunities. Third, in a competition, there are pressures to achieve success, and mistakes are not valued, which is not a good situation for learning. To learn, you must be allowed to make mistakes, and you cannot focus solely on the outcome of the task. In other words, in a one-versus-one situation in practice, you may be willing to try a new move that you have been working on. You might try the new move and you might fail at it. But, it's not a big deal. This is practice, and you are supposed to try new things and you will have another opportunity to try the move again because it is practice! In a competition, either you might be unwilling to try the new move at all or you might get discouraged if you try the move and are not successful. To improve and to make this new move a part of your skill set, you have to practice it repeatedly against strong competition and in situations when your success or failure at the move does not have any meaningful consequences.

The most frequent and best exposure to high levels of competition that you can get are through training with the other athletes on your team. These are the people who will be practicing with you regularly, so you can have somewhat constant exposure to challenging competition through practicing with and against your teammates. Thus, another consideration you must make in picking a team to play for is to try to find a team or group that is made up of other athletes who will challenge you on a daily basis.

With respect to your teammates, you must also consider their motivations for playing. If the team is made up of athletes who also have goals of competing at a high level, then they will be motivated to work hard in practice and to continue to improve. If the team is made up of athletes who are content to compete at their current level, then they may not be as motivated to work hard in practice and may not be focused on improving. Clearly, if you are motivated to improve every day, it will help if your teammates feel the same way.

## Will You Get Playing Time?

Fourth, will you get the opportunity to perform in competitions for this coach, and is that important to you? This question illustrates the fine line that exists in choosing a team full of other skilled, motivated athletes versus choosing a team where you will have the opportunity to perform in competitive situations on a regular basis. I just made the point that the repetitions that you get through practice will contribute the most to your development in your sport. But performing in competitive situations is also important to your development. If you can find a team where you are challenged every day in practice and can also perform in competitive situations, that is likely to be the ideal situation.

That being said, there are players who reach very high levels of play by devoting themselves to their improvement as practice players but who get very little game time in real competitions. Matt Cassell of the National Football League (NFL) is a great example. Matt was the second-string quarterback at the University of Southern California for four years. During those four years, he took only a handful of snaps in real games. But Matt was drafted into the NFL and got the opportunity to be the starting quarterback in sixteen games for the New England Patriots in 2008. Matt's performance was exceptional—he became only the fifth quarterback ever to have more than 400 passing yards in back-to-back games, and he was the first quarterback since 1970 to have more than 400 passing yards and more than 60 rushing yards in a single game. Clearly, Matt continued to develop his skills as a quarterback through his four years as a backup quarterback in college and was ready to perform at a high level when given the chance as a professional football player.

The key question for you to consider is how you will respond if you are not given the opportunity to perform in competitive situations. I know of many athletes who lost their motivation to continue working hard to improve themselves when they felt that their efforts were not noticed or rewarded by their coaches. I also know athletes who were able to maintain their high levels of motivation when they were not getting a chance to perform in competitions—in fact, some were motivated even more when they were striving to get a chance to compete.

If playing time is important to you but the coach doesn't give you the chance to play, you need to either use this as a motivational tool or look for a team where you will get a chance to play.

You may need to consider how this balance will affect you when you are selecting a team. Although you are likely to improve substantially over the course of a season in which you are giving great effort during practice, practicing against skilled teammates, and receiving attention and instruction from the coach, you need to consider how you will respond if you do not get the chance to perform in competition. This assessment may represent the hardest decision that you have to make with respect to choosing a team. For example, you may be able to "play up" to an older age group or to a team that competes at a higher level, and this opportunity will be invaluable in terms of your skill development; but if you don't eventually get the opportunity to participate in competitions and this is important to you, then it might be better for you to stay at your own age-group level or on a team where the opportunity to perform in competition is more equitable across athletes. This decision may be truly difficult to make. Playing with other athletes who are not as skillful or as motivated as yourself means that you might get lots of opportunities in competition, but you will not be challenged to improve on a daily basis in practice. Conversely, joining a team with other athletes who are more skillful than you and who are equally motivated means that you will be challenged regularly in practice, but you won't get the same amount of exposure to competitive events. There is no right or wrong answer as to what to do, but the ideal situation is one where you are on a team where the range of skills includes your own (that is, you are somewhere in the middle of the pack skillwise). This way you will be challenged by the better athletes on a regular basis, but you will also get the chance to participate in competitive events so that you learn to perform well tactically and technically when the pressure is on.

## Does Your Style Match the Coach's Style?

A final consideration is whether or not your style of interactions and playing and practicing matches that of the coach. There are many coaches who can help you improve as a player, but the amount that you improve will depend partly on how well you and your coach "fit" together. As an example, Mike Krzyzewski and Bobby Knight are two college basketball coaches who have achieved high levels of success with their teams. Both coaches are masters of the game of basketball and are able to foster the development of their players. However, the coaching styles of these two Coach K's is dramatically different. Coach Knight is incredibly demanding and has a temper that is evident in practices and games. In contrast, Coach Krzyzewski believes firmly that his role as a coach is to provide a climate where his athletes are free to experiment with their performance, where winning is not everything, and where his athletes feel compassion and unconditional support from their coach. While both coaches have won national championships with their teams, the difference in styles is such that athletes with certain personalities will work better with each coach. In other words, certain players might develop best playing for Coach Knight and others might develop best playing for

Coach Krzyzewski. If you have the choice between two coaches who are equally talented, then you will probably be much more content if you select the coach whose style of interacting with others and coaching matches your own preference and style.

## KEY POINTS

- Although you might not always have the freedom to select a team and coach to play for, when you do have this opportunity, the choice can have important implications for your personal development as an athlete.
- There are several points you should consider in selecting a team and a coach. These include
  - the coach's knowledge of the sport/game;
  - the ability of the coach to relay his/her knowledge of the game to the players;
  - the motivation level and skill level of the team members;
  - your chances of getting the opportunity to perform in competitions and your evaluation of how important this is to you; and
  - the "fit" between the coach's style and your own preferences and style.

# Identifying a Coach and Team to Train With

When you are trying to identify a coach to train with, you should spend some time gathering information about the coach and the athletes that he or she works with. To do this, you should consider meeting the coach, observing a training session, and talking to athletes who have worked with this coach. Use the worksheet provided to help guide you in collecting information that will be relevant in your decision-making process.

## *Notes Regarding a Potential Coach*

**POTENTIAL COACH'S NAME**

_____

**COACH'S KNOWLEDGE OF THE GAME**
Certifications?

Played at a high level?

Coached at a high level?

**COACH'S ABILITY TO RELAY KNOWLEDGE**
Observation of session?

Feelings of players?

Success of coach's players at the next level?

## TEAMMATES

Observation of session. Do teammates support one another?
Do they work hard? Do they listen to the coach?

Accomplishments of the team?

## PLAYING TIME

If this is a competitive team, am I good enough (or realistically able
to become good enough) to get playing time?

If I won't get playing time, can I remain motivated enough to
benefit from playing on this team?

## STYLE

What style of coaching does the coach use? Does he or she ask
questions of the players? Does he or she seem to give positive
feedback?

# Mental Toughness

Now that we have briefly considered physical characteristics, technical skills, tactical abilities, and the selection of a coach and team, it is time to move to the heart of this book, which is the development of mental toughness. Mental toughness is an all-encompassing term that describes the characteristics of a person who is able to commit day in and day out to training for excellence and who is able to perform at the top of his or her game in the face of stress, distractions, and even bad luck. Mental toughness describes the tennis player who battles back from one set down to win the match. It describes the volleyball player who regains a starting position on the team after undergoing surgery to repair a torn knee ligament. It describes the baseball team that performs at 100% even when facing a team that should be easily beaten. Similarly, it describes the field hockey team that fights and scrapes to win a game that it was expected to lose miserably. Finally, mental toughness describes the athlete who gets up early every morning to get in a training run, who makes healthy eating choices, who skips a social event to study, and who practices alone or with the team for hours each day and for days each week to achieve his or her goals.

Arguably, in today's sporting events, mental toughness is the characteristic that most clearly separates successful from unsuccessful athletes. In fact, Bill Russell (a former NBA basketball player who was most valuable player for the league five times) described this well when he said, "Concentration and mental toughness are the margins of victory." Because most athletes know how to get themselves physically ready to compete and because most have had access to appropriate skills training and tactical expertise, many coaches believe that the single most critical

Mental toughness is evident in the performance of athletes who refuse to let distractions, stress, or bad luck get to them.

attribute that determines success or failure is mental toughness. In fact, that is one of the main premises of this book—that mental toughness is the margin of victory needed to help you reach your potential in sport.

So what is mental toughness? How do you know if you are mentally tough? You can see mental toughness displayed in a number of ways. Mental toughness may be evident in the willingness of an athlete to respond to criticisms of his or her performance, in the ability of an athlete to stick to a more difficult training regimen than his or her closest competitor, in the commitment of an athlete who fights back from an injury, or in the ability of an athlete to maintain focus at the end of a grueling competitive event. Mental toughness is evident every time that you push yourself a little harder, that you persevere in the face of adversity, that you rebound from a difficult experience, and that you perform well under pressure. If you want to increase your chances of playing at the highest level, then you need to develop your mental toughness. And just like with physical fitness, technical skills, and tactical abilities, practice is the key to the development of mental toughness.

The mental toughness techniques described here will supplement your physical abilities and your talent in your sport to help you to be a better performer. The central thing to remember is that learning about these skills is only a first step. The next step is to incorporate the practice of these mental skills into your training regimen. To benefit fully from these mental skills, you must practice them on a regular basis so that they become second nature and so that they help you to consistently perform at a nearly automatic level in your sport. This idea of performing at a nearly automatic level is important because by doing so, you will be able to perform well in the face of pressure, adversity, injury, and all other manner of challenges. Mentally tough athletes use psychological skills to ensure that they maintain a consistently high level of performance from competition to competition. Finding time to practice your mental skills is not difficult. Mental skills can be practiced while you are training physically for your sport, but they can also be practiced at times when you are not physically training. That is, you can practice your mental skills to benefit performance in other settings (like when you commit to excellence in the classroom), and you can even practice mental skills when you are not performing any activity at all (like when you are simply resting or riding the bus to school). So now let's turn to the real goal of this book and talk about the skills that will help you develop mental toughness and that will ultimately help you to reach your potential in your sport.

# Identify Mental Toughness Characteristics from an Interview

Much of the information that is presented in this book has been used by elite athletes who have incorporated it into their training and preparations for competition. If you pay close attention to the answers that athletes and coaches give when interviewed after competition, you will notice many of these techniques at work. Listen to an interview of an athlete or coach (or conduct one yourself if possible) and see if you can identify any of the following characteristics of a mentally tough athlete.

1. Focuses on things that are controllable; does not focus on things that are not controllable.

2. Uses positive attributions.

    a. "Takes Credit" when explaining a successful event.

    b. Explains a lack of success as being due to "Poor Process."

3. Uses goal-setting techniques.

4. Understands the importance of managing energy levels.

5. Uses mental imagery to prepare for competition.

6. Focuses on process rather than outcome.

7. Uses a pre-performance routine or mini-routines to help make performance consistent and automatic.

8. Has confidence in his or her ability.

9. Understands the importance of balance in sport and in life, but is willing to make sacrifices to achieve his or her goals.

10. Has battled back from disappointment.

# 7. Goal Setting

Are you surprised to learn that athletes like Tiger Woods and Andre Agassi knew they wanted to be professional athletes from the time they were really young? In fact, Michael Owen, a professional soccer player who currently plays for Newcastle United, said that he knew he wanted to be a professional soccer player from the time he was a small child and that he started working toward that goal in a serious way very early. Owen said, "I've always had this goal [to be a professional soccer player], known what's best for me, and steered clear of the things that would do any harm to myself. I've always thought of myself as a professional-to-be. Even when I was a ten-year-old, I was eating good food and going to bed at a sensible hour. I've always been that way."

Whether your ultimate goal is to be a professional athlete, to play for your high school varsity team, or to earn a place on a traveling youth team, one thing is clear: it is important to identify your goal early, to create a blueprint for getting there, and to begin working toward your goal in a committed fashion. To use an analogy, if your dream is to go to Ft. Lauderdale for a vacation, your chances of reaching that dream are better if you have access to a car (the ability), some gas (the drive), and a good map (the directions). If any one of these is missing, then my guess is that you're not going to spend your vacation on the beach! Once you've identified your ultimate goal, the technique of goal setting will help you to put yourself in a position to reach it.

## What Is Goal Setting?

Generally speaking, goal setting is a technique that you can use to help you realize your potential and put yourself in a position to achieve your ultimate goal. Goal setting includes identifying both short-term and mid-term goals that are designed to help you reach your long-term goal. Goal setting is effective because it helps you develop a blueprint that will lead you to your long-term goal, encourages you to focus your energy on short- and mid-term goals, and provides a reward system to keep you motivated as you move forward.

The first step in goal setting is to identify the ultimate goal that you would like to reach. What I mean by ultimate goal is your dream of who you want to become. The ultimate goal (or dream) is one that is likely to be in the distant future and challenging to attain. Although this long-term goal should be realistic, it should also demonstrate a high degree of confidence in your ability to work toward that dream. It should be an achievement that you feel it is your destiny and mission to try to attain. An example is the thirteen-year-old athlete who says, "It is my goal to play volleyball on my high school varsity team," or the seventeen-year-old tennis player who says, "It is my dream to play tennis profession-ally." Both of these ultimate goals are wonderful, and they are certainly worth trying to reach; but you must also remember that simply having a goal won't get you there. *Wanting* to be a varsity athlete or a profes-sional tennis player clearly is not enough. If that were all that there was to it, then there would be a million professional athletes, because this is the dream of a million young athletes!

So what differentiates the thirteen-year-old who reaches his or her ul-timate goal from the thirteen-year-old who does not? Why do you know the name Tiger Woods but you've never heard of Noplan McGee? Well, there are a lot of reasons for this, but one key is the ability to effectively use goal setting to put yourself in a position to attain your ultimate goal. Tiger Woods and Noplan McGee had equal talent, ability, and access to resources as children; but Tiger Woods used goal setting to help him to achieve his ultimate goal, while Noplan McGee never developed a blue-print for success. As a result, Tiger Woods began accomplishing his goals in golf while Noplan McGee never realized his potential in sport. So let's talk more about goal setting, because this is a key component in your quest to reach your potential in sport.

If you've identified an ultimate goal that is realistic yet challenging, that you're committed to achieving, and that you feel motivated to work toward, the next question to ask yourself is "What do I need to do to get there?" If you can identify the proper steps that lead to your dream and you work to attain each of these steps, then ultimately you will put yourself in a position to reach the dream.

Let me provide a visual example based on the ambition of wanting to play for your high school varsity soccer team (see illustration on next page). "Playing varsity soccer" is your ultimate goal, so it is like a high platform that you want to reach. As a thirteen-year-old, the platform of "playing varsity soccer" seems so high that you cannot possibly reach it without a series of lower-level platforms and ladders to help you get there. The key for you is to create the blueprint showing the achievements that will be necessary to put yourself in a position to reach your ultimate dream.

You must first identify some achievements that are logical stepping-stones on the path to your ultimate dream. These achievements are your mid-term goals and represent the lower-level platforms that give you a new base of support for another series of ladders and platforms. So the lowest-level platforms on your way to becoming a member of the varsity soccer team might be "honing my technical skills," "increasing my fitness," and "enhancing my mental toughness." These platforms support a ladder that will help you to reach the next platform, which is "playing on a competitive club team." This mid-term goal then supports you as you move toward your next goal of "playing on the junior varsity soccer team." Finally, this platform supports your ability to climb up the last ladder, which gets you to your ultimate goal of making varsity at your high school.

So now you've got the idea. You've got an ultimate goal (the high platform) that you're committed to reaching, and you understand that to reach that goal you're going to have to identify mid-term goals (lower-level platforms) that you'll need to reach to help you get to your dream. Now, you've probably recognized that the identification of these mid-term goals is still only a starting point, because reaching each of these will require a separate ladder with its own steps. In other words, just identifying your lower-level platforms is not enough to ensure that you will actually reach them. You must still identify the necessary smaller steps that will get you to each of these platforms. You will develop a combination of short-term and mid-term goals to reach your dream. Sound like a lot of work? Well, it does require some thinking and some

Reaching your dream will not be possible unless you first achieve a series of short-term goals (ladder rungs) and mid-term goals (lower-level platforms).

effort, but didn't you just tell me that you were committed to reaching your ultimate goal? To reach an ultimate goal does take work and planning, but if you're committed to reaching your goal, then we're ready to get started.

## Guidelines for Goal Setting

Let's talk more about the technique of goal setting so that you can begin to clearly identify the platforms and ladders that will take you to your dream. These platforms and ladders serve several purposes. First, if they are properly developed, they provide a blueprint that will lead you to your dream (this is our plan). Second, they give you a ruler by which to measure your progress toward your dream (this lets you know if you're making progress). Third, they help you to experience the reward of reaching each of the lower-level platforms (time for a cookie!).

## Make the Blueprint

The first step in goal setting is to identify the mid-term goals that are logical steps on your path to your ultimate goal and then to figure out the smaller steps needed to reach each mid-term goal. At this stage, you'll benefit from asking for the assistance of a coach, parent, or older athlete. Ideally, this person should have experience in your sport, thus serving as an architect who can provide valuable insights as you design your blueprint. As the architect, this person will help you identify all of the important lower-level platforms and correctly construct your ladders to include the important steps needed to reach each of those platforms. This person will also help you understand where you are now relative to your dream. In other words, it is extremely important to be aware of where you are now relative to your ultimate goal, because you don't want the first platforms to be so out of reach that your ladders are too long and unstable. Additionally, having a stair-step system in place is critically important because accomplishing your short-term goals will give you positive reinforcement and evidence that you are making progress toward your ultimate goal.

Let me give you a non-sport example of how the "architect" can help with developing an effective goal-setting plan. Karl has never traveled abroad, and he dreams of traveling to England the summer after he graduates from high school. To achieve this goal, Karl develops a blueprint. As you read about Karl's goal-setting plan, keep your eye out for the important missing step that would prevent Karl from reaching his dream.

The lower-level platforms that Karl has identified include making a travel plan and earning enough money for the trip. To reach the mid-term goal of making his travel plan for the trip, Karl constructs a ladder that includes the following steps: meeting with a travel agent to explain that he would like to see as much of the country as possible, searching the Internet for information about travel in England, and going to the library to get books on travel in England. Karl also has a plan to reach his other mid-term goal of raising enough money to pay for the trip by the end of his senior year. The steps to achieving this goal include mowing lawns for his neighbors, completing additional chores around the house for pay from his parents, and selling some of his CD and DVD collection on E-bay. The second level of platforms in the blueprint includes purchasing airplane and train tickets for his trip and making reservations for lodging. Notice, however, that these second-level platforms cannot be reached until the lower-level goals have been accomplished, since the lower-level platforms provide key support for the mid-term goals. In other words, how can Karl purchase tickets if he hasn't reached the mid-term goal of earning enough money for the trip?

After constructing his blueprint, Karl shares his dream and his goal-setting plan with a family friend, Patti, who has done a lot of traveling, to make sure that the ladders and platforms are appropriate for reaching his dream. Patti's own travel experiences make her the perfect architect to help Karl review his blueprint. Patti immediately notices that Karl has left out one crucial step, without which Karl will not be able to reach his dream of going to England. Did you catch it, too? Think about everything that you would need to be able to travel abroad. See if you can figure out the key piece that Karl left out of his plan. Did you figure it out?

The key step for traveling abroad that Karl has left out of his goal-setting plan is getting a passport. Karl's dream was good, his blueprint for success was well thought out, and he was committed to climbing the ladders to reach each platform in pursuit of his ultimate dream. But if Karl failed to obtain a passport, his trip would have been impossible and he would not have reached his dream. This example demonstrates how important it is to have an experienced friend, coach, or teammate review your goals to ensure that your goal-setting plan is appropriately designed and contains every step necessary for you to reach your dream.

At the end of this chapter are exercises to help you to develop your blueprint for success. This would be a good time to take a look at these worksheets to get an idea of the steps I'll be asking you to take once you've read all of the guidelines for goal setting.

### Write Down Your Goals

You should always write down your goals when designing your plan. Writing down your goals is important for two reasons. First, you see your blueprint to success. These written goals will provide you with an easy way to evaluate your progress so that you can experience the rewards of putting each rung of each ladder in place and the joy of knowing that you have reached each of the lower-level platforms. Second, by writing down your goals, you make a contract with yourself. In other words, by simply writing down your goals, you are demonstrating your commitment to working toward these goals. In fact, you should write a sentence at the end of the goals that says, "I am committed to giving 100% to achieve these goals," and then sign your name below this sentence. Keep in mind that reaching your ultimate dream will be hugely rewarding and that by using goal setting, all of your hard work will be effectively focused toward this achievement.

## Post Your Goals

Once you have written down your goals, it is important that you put them in a place where you can see them on a regular basis. Post them on the refrigerator or on your bathroom mirror. You don't want to look in the back corner of your desk drawer five years from now and find your blueprint sitting there with the goals forgotten. Some people use this easy excuse when they fail to reach their dream. They take the step of writing down their goals but then conveniently forget them. Then, when they don't reach their goal, they blame their failure on the goal-setting technique not being effective. Don't fall into this trap. If you are serious about trying to reach your dream, then you've got to stay committed throughout the entire process. Once you have developed your blueprint, post it where you can see it every day and use it to guide your efforts and to evaluate your progress toward your dream.

As mentioned earlier, Tiger Woods effectively used goal setting to help him reach his dream. He provides the perfect example of how posting goals and looking at them daily can contribute to reaching dreams. As a young athlete, Tiger used another highly accomplished golfer's achievements to set a benchmark for what he wanted to accomplish. When Tiger was setting his goals, Jack Nicklaus was the best player in the world and was considered to be the best golfer who ever played the game. Tiger decided that beating the best was his goal, and he used the age at which Jack accomplished each of his personal achievements to help guide his own goals. Tiger wrote down Jack's achievements and the age at which Jack accomplished each of them and posted the list next to his bathroom mirror. Then Tiger set his own short-term goals designed to help him to achieve each of these feats. It is a tribute to Tiger's talent, goal-setting abilities, work ethic, mental toughness, and commitment that he has achieved many of these same goals, and at younger ages than Jack did.

### Share Your Goals with Supportive People

As a third guideline in goal setting, share your goals with people who will be supportive of you. There are people in your life who can help you work toward reaching your goals and who can support you in a variety of ways. These people probably include your parents, siblings, friends, teammates, and coaches. I would encourage you to let these people know about your dream and about your goal-setting plan. This may be especially necessary with your parents, who provide crucial support (like transportation to practice and games and money for equipment and coaching) to allow you to pursue your dream. It is also important to share your goals with friends, siblings, and teammates who are supportive of you. Although these people are not likely to pay for your equipment, they can provide invaluable help through their emotional support (by encouraging you to practice hard and cheering you up when times are tough). Sharing your goals with your coaches is also important, because your coaches can help you refine your goals and pursue opportunities for additional training and competition that will help you reach your goals.

There are also people who may not be supportive of you, and you would be wise to keep your goals from these people, as they might make fun of you or even work to sabotage your efforts. For example, when Michael was a senior in high school, he told his friend Steve that his dream was to make the U.S. Olympic team. Steve began to make fun of Michael and tease him for having such a lofty dream. Steve even went so far as to ask Michael to go out partying with their friends on Fridays before competitions, and he would tease Michael by saying, "Well, you're good enough to think you're going to be an Olympian, I'm sure you'll still play well if you come out and party with us!" Obviously, sharing his dream with Steve was not a good idea, because Steve could not support Michael's efforts toward reaching his dream.

### Make Your Goals Specific, Measurable, Action-oriented, Realistic, and Timely (SMART)

A fourth guideline for goal setting is that your goals should be written in a way that will allow you to evaluate your progress, reward the small accomplishments, and understand the time frame in which the goals need to be accomplished. Many sport psychologists describe this as using SMART goals. SMART is an acronym to help you remember that your goals should be **S**pecific, **M**easurable, **A**ction-oriented, **R**ealistic, and **T**imely. In the example of Karl using goal setting to help him reach his goal of traveling to England in the summer, he had a goal of raising enough money for the trip by mowing lawns and doing chores. Although there is nothing wrong with this goal, it is not very specific or measurable. For instance, how much money is "enough"? How can Karl direct his efforts effectively when the goal is written in this vague fashion? Karl's goal can be improved if he specifies exactly how much money he needs. Karl will have to figure out how much the airplane and train tickets, lodging, food, other travel expenses, entertainment, gifts, and other odds and ends will cost so that he can include this in his goal. Once Karl has all of this figured out, he can write a much better goal by saying that he needs to raise $2,200. This is a much-improved goal because it is specific and measurable. But a new criticism of this goal is that it's written in a fashion that may be a bit intimidating because of the sheer size of the goal. In other words, as written, this goal might seem unrealistic and feel impossible to attain, and it might not have the desired motivating effect on Karl's behavior. So to further improve this goal, Karl could break it down even further and add a timeline so that the goal will feel more realistic. For example, Karl could divide it into two goals: "I will raise $1,200 by February so I can purchase the airplane and train tickets" and "I will raise an additional $1,000 by June for the other expenses." Now the remaining shortcoming is that these two goals are not action-oriented. In other words, what is Karl supposed to *do* to meet these goals? What behaviors will he adopt? What steps will he take? As written, it's not clear how Karl will accomplish these goals. So the last step is to make the goals more action-oriented. To further improve his goals, Karl could write the two goals as follows: "I will do the chores at my house on weekends and will house-sit for the Lewis family in January to raise $1,200 by February so I can purchase the airplane and train tickets" and "This spring, I will mow the Goldfarbs', Pearsons', and Wagners' lawns every week to raise $1,200 by June." These are examples of goals that follow the SMART acronym—they are specific, measurable, action-oriented, realistic, and timely.

In sport, an example of a goal that could be improved is "I will practice hard." Although this is obviously a good thing to try to achieve and makes sense in relation to your blueprint for success, it is not written in a way that allows you to judge your progress. In other words, how will you know if you have practiced "hard"? How will you monitor your progress on this goal? A more concrete goal is "I will work hard in practice by committing to hitting ground strokes for 30 minutes per day for 5 days per week." This goal is better because it has all of the components of a SMART goal. Thus, you can gauge your efforts toward this goal on a weekly basis. That way, if the goal is actually too hard or too easy, you can adjust it to match your needs and to ensure your steady improvement in the sport. This example leads us to the next guideline.

### Be Flexible and Willing to Adjust Your Goals

Another important consideration regarding goal setting is that you should be flexible in your goals and should review them on a regular basis to make adjustments as needed. For example; you might have just completed a gymnastics competition over the weekend and your floor routine was solid but your performance on the bars let you down. As a result, you adjust your goals so that you will work on your floor routine only three days per week and will increase the amount of practice time that you devote to the bars so that you work on this apparatus at every practice session.

Occasionally you may also need to adjust your expectations slightly in response to suddenly changing situations. If, for example, you come down with the flu, sprain your ankle, or have an extraordinarily demanding week at school, you may not be able to meet your short-term goals for a particular week and you might have to adjust your goals. You should feel comfortable when you need to do this and should definitely not feel disappointed or frustrated. It is okay occasionally to modify your blueprint in response to things like feedback from a coach, making more rapid progress than you expected, and uncontrollable events that hinder your progress. However, don't let this idea of flexibility and adjustment serve as an excuse for not working hard toward your goals. Be wary of the attractive trap of thinking that every week has challenges that make it acceptable to shortchange your efforts. And don't let a minor setback be your excuse for giving up on your goal-setting plan. Once you have set up your blueprint and have committed yourself to it, don't let daily hassles, minor stressors, or even seemingly large setbacks stand in the way of achieving your dream. It is important to remember that your blueprint for success is a long-range plan designed to help you to reach your ultimate goal; minor bumps in the road are not valid excuses for not achieving your goals. I think it is fair to say that every person who has achieved an ultimate dream had to fight through setbacks, disappointments, and weeks when things just did not seem to be going right (see Chapter 17). If you want to reach your long-term goal, you will have to be the kind of person who can fight these battles.

The experience of my friend Jim provides a great example of being flexible with your goals. Jim played soccer for Brandeis University and was the star of his team. During his junior year, Jim set goals for himself that included being one of the team's top assist-makers, being one of the top scorers, and improving his defensive abilities. Halfway through his junior year, Jim was on track to reach these goals. But then the unthinkable happened. In a game in which Jim's team was ahead 3-0, Jim was working hard in the penalty box to get the ball to his right foot, which was his best for shooting. He gave a fake to lose his defender and cut hard to the right—then *pop* went his knee. Jim had torn his ACL (anterior cruciate ligament, an important ligament in the knee that is often injured in sport). He was out for the rest of his junior season. How did Jim react? He clearly was not able to reach his goals for his junior year and, in fact, was not even able to play for the rest of the season. To Jim's credit, he completely modified his goals to match the situation. His new goals were to improve his ball skills with his left leg, to improve his strength in both legs, and to improve his understanding of the game and of defensive responsibilities. Jim then committed himself to working hard in the training room to increase his strength. He attended every practice, and while the team was practicing, he either worked with the ball with his left foot on his own on the sideline or he sat with the coach to learn more about the tactics of the game. When Jim returned to the field his senior year, he was a much-improved player. His understanding of team defense was vastly improved, his skill with his left foot was so much better that he could score equally well with either foot, and his strength was such that he was at less risk of injury his senior year. Jim went on to be the leading scorer for his team and for the league that season, and he was the third-highest assist-maker in the league.

Another great example of a player who had to adjust his goals and to maintain his focus in the face of huge disappointment is Jeff Agoos. Jeff played in seven games for the U.S. men's soccer team in 1991 and was a starting defender in twenty matches in 1993. He was training hard to reach his goal to be named a member of the 1994 World Cup team, but

Jeff was one of the last players to be cut from that team. It was reported that, to express his grief and disappointment, Jeff burned his training gear shortly after hearing the news (something I'm sure he is not proud of). However, Jeff displayed incredible mental toughness and persistence over the next several years by continuing to work hard toward his dream of playing again for the national team and of playing for a World Cup. In 1997 Jeff played the most minutes of any player in the international games that helped qualify the United States for the 1998 World Cup. In 1998 Jeff was named a member of the World Cup team, but he never got to play a single minute in any game. Four years later, as a result of his continuing hard work, commitment to excellence, and development as a player, Jeff was named to the 2002 World Cup team and started in three games for the United States. This is a great example of how important it is to be flexible with your goals, to maintain your commitment to excellence, and to adjust your goals with changing situations. If you stick with it, you can ultimately reach your dreams—great job Jeff!

### Set Up a Reward System

You should set up a reward system so that you get reinforcement for climbing the rungs of the ladders to reach each platform. This guideline is important because the rungs of each ladder may consist of goals that are not very motivating in and of themselves. For example, during the three months between tennis tournaments, meeting your short-term goals of hitting ground strokes for 30 minutes per day for 5 days per week, running 2 miles every day at an 8-minute pace, and using imagery for 15 minutes per day prior to every practice may *not* be very rewarding at the time. There are some players who just love to practice; but for most players, the repetition of practice can become boring, and these players may get frustrated with working so hard with no immediate rewards. So to help with this situation, you should incorporate rewards into your program to congratulate yourself for sticking to your plan and reaching the rungs of the ladders that will take you to the next platform. For example, after meeting the above-mentioned short-term goals for a month, maybe you reward yourself by buying some new iTunes or enjoying a movie with a friend. This type of reward for your hard work will help you stay motivated for the next phase of your plan. As a caution, however, realize that when you set up a reward system, your rewards should be compatible with your goals. In other words, it would not be sensible for your reward to be taking a week off from practice or staying up all night with friends watching television and playing video games. Either of these might actually set you back in your progress toward reaching your goals.

In summary, goal setting is a very useful technique that will benefit your performance in several ways. First, the process of setting goals forces you to develop your blueprint of ladders and platforms that you will need to reach on the way to your ultimate goal. In other words, by taking the time to design a blueprint for success, you are taking the first step toward the realization of your dream. Second, the platforms that you have identified give you a way to measure your progress. If you use goal setting only to write down your ultimate goal, you will not have any short-term achievements that can help you to stay motivated. Identifying the lower-level platforms gives you the ability to self-monitor and to judge and reward your improvements and gains over a relatively short period of time. Third, if you have designed your blueprint appropriately and if you reach each of the platforms that support your ultimate dream, you will put yourself in the best possible position to have an opportunity to attain the dream. You might have noticed that I did not say that you will definitely reach your dream. This is because it is important to recognize that using goal setting will allow you to be completely prepared and at the top of your game, but you still have only a chance to be successful. Unfortunately, the achievement of your ultimate dream is only partially under your control (see Chapter 11, in which I talk about things that are controllable and things that are not controllable relative to your performance). However, goal setting is a valuable technique that you can use so that you are as prepared as possible and have the opportunity to be successful. The value of goal setting is clearly described by Kieran Perkins, one of the world's best long-distance swimmers, who captured the relationship between goal setting and being your best when he said, "Being your best is not so much about overcoming the barriers other people place in front of you as it is about overcoming the barriers we place in front of ourselves. It has nothing to do with how many times you win or lose. It has no relation to where you finish in a race or whether you break world records. But it does have everything to do with having the vision to dream, the courage to recover from adversity, and the determination never to be shifted from your goals."

• Goal setting is a tool that should be used to direct your efforts toward reaching your sport potential.

• Goal setting is effective because it helps you develop a blueprint for success and gives you a means to evaluate and reward your progress toward your ultimate dream.

• When writing your goals, you should follow these guidelines:

  ° Define your ultimate dream and then develop a blueprint to success that consists of lower-level platforms and ladders that will get you to your dream.

  ° Ask someone with experience in your sport to review your blueprint.

  ° Write down your goals, write a statement at the bottom expressing your commitment to these goals, and then sign the statement.

  ° Post your goals where you can see them daily.

  ° Share your goals with people who can be supportive and ask them to assist you in reaching these goals.

  ° Make your goals SMART: Specific, Measurable, Action-oriented, Realistic, and Timely. This process will make the attainment of the goals manageable and will give you a way to judge whether or not you are reaching these goals.

  ° Recognize that you may need to be flexible with your goals and adjust your goals as necessary.

  ° Create a reward system that gives you reinforcement for reaching your short-term goals. Use rewards that are compatible with your goals.

• Remember that achieving your short-term and long-term goals will put you in the best possible position to have the opportunity to reach your ultimate dream.

# Creating a Blueprint to Help You Reach Your Goals

What you need for this exercise: a pen or pencil and the worksheet pages that follow. The worksheets include an example sheet and blank sheets titled Organizing Sheet and Goal-Setting Sheet. Use the example worksheets to help you understand how to use the blank worksheets.

1. Write down your dream (ultimate goal) at the top of both worksheets in capital letters (be bold here—write down your real and optimistic dream for your future).

2. Across the top of both sheets, write down the series of lower-level platforms (mid-term goals) that you'll need to reach as stepping-stones on the way to achieving your dream.

3. On the left side of your Organizing Sheet, write down the names of some people who can help you to reach your goals. These should be people who will be supportive of you and who have information (related to how to be successful in your sport) that will be helpful to you.

4. Find a time to talk one-on-one with each of these supportive people. Tell them your dream and ask them for specific advice as to how to reach this dream. Tell them that you are trying to develop a "blueprint" that will consist of a series of platforms and ladders to help you to reach your dream. On the right side of your Organizing Sheet, make notes from these conversations.

5. After you have compiled the information from your supporters, go to your Goal-Setting Sheet and write down the short-term goals that will serve as the rungs of the ladders that get you to each lower-level platform (mid-term goal).

6. At the bottom of the Goal-Setting Sheet, write the following sentence: "I am committed to giving 100% to achieve these goals." Then sign your name below this sentence.

7. Post your Goal-Setting Sheet in a place where you will see it every day. This could be beside your bathroom mirror or in your school locker.

8. Look over your Goal-Setting Sheet each day and work hard to attain your short-term goals (the rungs on the ladder).

9. Use the reward system described in this chapter to help you stay motivated toward reaching your goals.

10. Every month, review the Goal-Setting Sheet and adjust it as necessary based on your ability to climb the rungs of the ladders and on your progress toward your first-level platforms.

## *Organizing Sheet Example*

**MY ULTIMATE GOAL:**  PLAY FOR MY HIGH SCHOOL VARSITY SOCCER TEAM

### THIRD-LEVEL PLATFORMS

1. Play on the junior varsity soccer team
2. Earn the opportunity to play in competitions
3. Continue to give 100% effort in practices and competitions

### SECOND-LEVEL PLATFORMS

1. Play on a competitive soccer club team
2. Earn the opportunity to play in the mid-field
3. Maintain focus and effort level during practices and games
4. Seek out challenges in practice to continue to develop

### FIRST-LEVEL PLATFORMS

1. Improve technical skills
2. Increase fitness
3. Enhance mental toughness
4. Gain in tactical understanding of the game

| SUPPORTERS | SUPPORTERS' SUGGESTIONS/ADVICE |
|---|---|
| 1. Coach Hunter | Be sure to improve technique on both sides (right and left) |
| | Fitness should include endurance, strength, and speed/quickness |
| 2. Lainey—HS soccer player | Be sure that your academics are still strong—commit to excellence in the classroom |
| | Seek out competition even in practices—pick good players to play with and against |

## Organizing Sheet

**MY ULTIMATE GOAL:** _____

**THIRD-LEVEL PLATFORMS**

1.                    2.                    3.                    4.

**SECOND-LEVEL PLATFORMS**

1.                    2.                    3.                    4.

**FIRST-LEVEL PLATFORMS**

1.                    2.                    3.                    4.

**SUPPORTERS**                    **SUPPORTERS' SUGGESTIONS/ADVICE**

1. _____        _____

                            _____

2. _____        _____

                            _____

3. _____        _____

                            _____

4. _____        _____

                            _____

5. _____        _____

                            _____

6. _____        _____

                            _____

# Goal-Setting Sheet Example

**MY ULTIMATE GOAL:** PLAY FOR MY HIGH SCHOOL VARSITY SOCCER TEAM

| FIRST-LEVEL PLATFORMS | Improve technical skills | Increase endurance, strength, speed/quickness | Enhance mental toughness | Gain in tactical understanding of the game |
|---|---|---|---|---|
| | 20 min / 3 × per week individual ball work | Give 100% during fitness activities in practice | Image practice behaviors during bus ride to school | Watch one televised game per week with Mom and analyze |
| LADDERS AND RUNGS | Talk to coach every Monday to assess weekly goals | Speed training 10 min / 3 × per week | Image skills during bus ride home | Talk to coach every Monday to assess my tactical goals |
| | 30 min each weekend shooting practice | Take weight-lifting class at school | Use pre-performance routine for every game | Do 2 extra chores/week to earn $ to attend D license coaching school |
| | Challenge the better players in 1-v-1 games | Run 3 miles / 8 min pace on weekend | Write in confidence book daily | Go to home varsity games with Dad to analyze |

*Goal-Setting Sheet*

MY ULTIMATE GOAL: _____

# Outcome Goals versus Process Goals

For developing mental toughness, this chapter is definitely one of the most important for young athletes to read. Outcome goals and process goals are categories or types of goals that athletes use to motivate themselves to perform. Just like it sounds, outcome goals are directed toward the outcome (win/loss) of a competition or event. A person who tends to adopt outcome goals is said to be outcome oriented. In contrast, process goals are directed toward the process or technique involved in a sport. A person who tends to adopt process goals is said to be process oriented. The information in this chapter is important because having a balance between outcome goals and process goals is crucial for success in athletics. Despite the importance of having a good balance in these types of goals, many young athletes focus almost exclusively on outcome goals and do not use process goals enough.

## 100% Outcome Orientation

At first glance, you might think that being 100% outcome oriented would be beneficial in competitive sport, because winning is usually the ultimate goal in a competition. You've probably heard the phrase "Winning isn't everything, it's the only thing," and Vince Lombardi's quote, "If winning isn't everything, why do they keep score?" Only the winners of the competition get the trophies, the pat on the back from their supporters, the opportunities to have sponsors, the television coverage, and the glory. But the irony here comes from the simple fact that being focused *only* on winning doesn't mean that you will be the winner. In fact, the winner of the competition usually will *not* be the person or team that has the strongest outcome orientation and is *only* focused on winning. The person or team that wins the competition usually has the right *balance* of an outcome orientation and a process orientation. Let me describe some of the reasons behind this conclusion, and you will begin to understand why this is true.

When you have a complete (or a strong) focus on outcome, your chances of being a "winner" and of playing at the highest level in your sport are slim, for a couple of reasons. First, if you are purely outcome oriented, then you will not respond well to losing. Given that losing is something that all athletes experience (and sometimes repeatedly), your ability to respond well to losses is critical and is a necessary component of being mentally tough. However, being purely outcome oriented suggests that you care only about winning and that you judge your success and failure in your sport based on whether or not you win the competition. If you win, then you see yourself as successful, which will help you to stay motivated to keep playing your sport. But if you lose, then you see yourself as a failure, and you may begin to lose your motivation to play. If you lose repeatedly, a really negative situation develops because you are so outcome oriented that you cannot fathom a reason to keep playing if you aren't getting the outcome you so strongly desire. In other words, if you are strongly outcome oriented, then your confidence, motivation, and enjoyment in sport revolve around winning the competitions. But it is not possible to win every competition, and ultimately you will experience a loss or a string of losses. When you experience these losses, if you are outcome oriented, your confidence, motivation, and enjoyment will be hurt; if this situation goes on long enough, you may ultimately drop out of the sport. Dean Smith, retired head coach of the University of North Carolina men's basketball team, captured this idea of the potential negative effects of losses on outcome-oriented players when he said, "If you make every game a life-and-death thing, you're going to have problems. You'll be dead a lot."

The second problem with a strong outcome orientation is that it influences the challenges that you are willing to face, and therefore it ultimately affects your ability to continue to improve in your sport. Imagine that you are a strongly outcome-oriented athlete and you have the opportunity to play one-versus-one with one of three people: your younger cousin, your slightly older cousin, or a professional player. If you are strongly outcome oriented and only care about winning, which opponent would you choose? If the most important thing to you is winning, clearly you would select the opponent whom you think you can beat. So your first choice would be to play against your younger cousin because the chance for victory is greatest against this weaker player. Do you see the problem with this over the long run? Does it jump out at you why this is not a good choice if your goal is to play at the highest level in your sport? If you get to make this choice every day, and every day you play against your younger cousin, then you might win every day, but you will not get any better as a player because you will not be challenged by the competition. Your confidence, motivation, and enjoyment will stay high because you are winning, but your level of performance will not improve because you are not challenging yourself to get better. And if you do not get better, then ultimately you are not going to reach your potential.

Okay, so as a strongly outcome-oriented athlete, your first choice was to play against your younger cousin. Now, between your slightly older cousin or the professional athlete, whom would you pick to play against next? Again, imagine that you are very outcome oriented. Between the older cousin and the professional athlete, whom would a very outcome-oriented player choose to play against? This answer is probably not as obvious. The strongly outcome-oriented player would choose the professional player. Does this choice make any sense? Well, it does because the outcome-oriented athlete knows that there is no chance to be successful against the professional, so when he or she loses to the professional athlete, the loss doesn't really mean anything. It doesn't hurt his or her confidence because there was never any chance of success against the professional athlete. The outcome-oriented person maintains high levels of confidence, motivation, and enjoyment because he or she doesn't care about the outcome if it is a foregone conclusion. But even by making this second choice, the outcome-oriented athlete will not improve. Imagine that you are playing basketball against NBA forward Carmelo Anthony. If he plays at 100%, my money says that you barely maintain possession of the ball and that you are lucky if you manage to get a shot off that hits the rim. So by making this second choice, the outcome-oriented athlete will again not have a chance to improve his or her game.

The last person the strongly outcome-oriented player would choose to compete against is the slightly older cousin. Do you understand why this is the last choice? If the outcome-oriented athlete plays against the slightly older cousin and loses, then the outcome-oriented athlete will interpret this as a very negative outcome. In other words, because there is a chance of success against the slightly older cousin, the meaning of a loss is extremely negative. To the outcome-oriented young athlete, a loss is a failure and means that he or she wasn't good enough. Playing against this relatively equal challenger puts the outcome-oriented athlete's confidence and motivation at risk. Therefore, the outcome-oriented athlete will tend to avoid this challenging level of competition to protect his or her confidence and motivation.

The ironic thing about this situation is that the athlete would improve the most by playing against the slightly older cousin on a regular basis because this level of challenge would result in improvements in technical and tactical abilities. However, this is the last choice that the outcome-oriented athlete would make. Although these are extreme examples, they indicate how an outcome orientation influences the level of competition that you might be willing to face. And, by choosing *not* to compete against the person who would provide the greatest level of competition, the outcome-oriented athlete misses out on opportunities to improve as a player.

As a real-life example of the effect of being strongly outcome oriented, let me tell you about Maria. I was coaching a team of thirteen-year-old girls, and there was a player named Maria who was exceptionally talented and whom I thought had real potential to be great. Because of this, I hoped that Maria would try out for a select traveling team for the fall season. I asked her if she was planning to try out for the team. Maria told me that she had given it a lot of thought and had decided not to try out for the select team. I was surprised and even a little upset because I thought Maria was wasting a great opportunity to improve her game. I said, "Maria, I think you are good enough to make the team. Why aren't you planning to try out?" Maria replied that she enjoyed being the best player on her current team and that she didn't think she could handle being one of the weaker players on a team, which is what she thought would happen if she were on the select team. This is a perfect example of how being strongly outcome oriented can have a negative impact on your potential. By being solely focused on beating others and winning, athletes limit their opportunities to improve as players. If Maria had played for the select team, she would have been exposed to high levels of competition on a daily basis in practice. She would have been challenged to improve. And she would have had the opportunity to grow as a player. Instead, because she was uncomfortable with the idea of not being the best player on the team, Maria was choosing to limit her opportunity for growth as a player and was content to maintain her position on her less-skilled club team.

Another consequence of being 100% outcome oriented is a failure to develop appropriate skills. In other words, if all you care about is the outcome, then you might be able to achieve the outcome without actually learning to perform necessary skills appropriately. Let me provide an example to illustrate what I mean. Recently I was playing outside with my four-year-old daughter, who was given a set of child-size golf clubs by some dear friends. She wanted to play with the golf clubs, so we put a ball on a tee and I showed her how to swing the club. As an experienced sport psychologist, I was doing the proper thing by encouraging her to focus only on process. There were no targets to aim at and I didn't care how far she hit the ball—I was only encouraging her to try to make contact with the ball. It didn't take long, however, for me to realize that even by simply focusing on contact, I was not doing a good job of ensuring success for my daughter or of really helping her focus on process. For a person who has picked up a golf club for the very first time, simply making contact with the ball is actually an outcome that can take away from the ability to focus on process. My daughter was clearly focused only on contacting the ball and wasn't paying any attention to the technique I had shown her for swinging the golf club. Instead of pulling the club back and swinging forward through the ball, she had figured out that by taking the club up over her head and hitting down on the ball, she was making contact more often. So she was using a technique that was completely wrong but was giving her the outcome that I'd mistakenly asked her to focus on. After figuring this out, I took the ball and tee away and said, "Let's focus on making the club just skim the surface of the grass so that it makes a nice whistling noise." The only way to do this is to use the appropriate golf motion, so once I took the ball away, she was able to focus on the process of properly swinging the golf club instead of on making contact with the ball. The point is that having an outcome orientation can limit your ability to perfect the movements necessary to perform a skill.

You can increase your likelihood of achieving some outcomes by performing the skill incorrectly. Clearly, this outcome focus will not help you to improve your technique!

## 100% Process Orientation

The opposite of someone who is 100% outcome oriented is the person who is 100% process oriented. This person is also not likely to be successful in sport. He or she doesn't care about winning but is only interested in improving his or her skill in the sport and in enjoying the activity. This person may become a very skillful athlete because of a continual focus on the process of skill development, but he or she is not likely to be successful in the sporting arena, where a level of commitment, effort, exertion, and risk taking may be necessary to achieve a winning outcome. Also, this person is not likely to put in the extra time and effort required to improve all aspects of his or her game because of the joy experienced from simply focusing on skill development. In other words, if I am not focused on outcome at all and simply enjoy practicing field hockey because I can see my skills improving, why would I want to join a competitive team that travels every weekend to compete in tournaments? Thus, people who are 100% process oriented and don't care about winning are not likely to have the competitive spirit necessary to be successful at high levels of sport. Instead, these individuals will always enjoy playing for fun and will tend to shy away from teams and events that emphasize competition.

## Balance of Outcome Orientation and Process Orientation

I want to emphasize that having a 100% outcome orientation or a 100% process orientation is not a bad thing. It simply means that you do not have an orientation that is most likely to help you to be successful at high levels of sport. In contrast, if you have a balance between an outcome orientation and a process orientation, you will be more mentally tough and will have the most appropriate orientation for sport success.

Let me give an example that emphasizes how a balance between the two orientations can contribute to a positive outcome. Phil Mickelson was playing in the 2002 U.S. Open—a very prestigious golf tournament. He was in third place at the beginning of the third day of competition, so he was certainly "in the hunt" to try to win the event and was focused on the potential victory. But on the first two holes that he played that day, Phil hit one shot over par (bogeyed) and had dropped to a tie for fifth place. At that point, Phil began thinking that he just needed to hit some good shots. He quit focusing on the outcome of the event. He quit focusing on trying to catch Sergio Garcia and Tiger Woods, who had started the day ahead of him. Instead, he began to focus on the process that would be required to play a good game of golf. He started thinking about things like his grip, his backswing, and his contact with the ball. What do you think happened next? You guessed it—Phil's performance began to improve. And when Phil's performance began to improve, Phil's outcome also started to improve—which is not surprising. Phil's focus on process resulted in him hitting one shot under par (birdying) the next three holes and getting himself back up to second place. This is a fantastic example of how focusing on the process or technique required

Having a balance between outcome and process and being able to shift your focus between the two will serve you well as you move through the ranks of your sport.

for performance ultimately will result in good performance (and, in fact, results in a good outcome for the immediate skill being performed). Although Phil did not win the tournament, his ability to balance his focus between process and outcome allowed him to improve his standing from fifth place to second place and put him in a position where winning the tournament was possible if his opponent failed to maintain a high level of play. Unfortunately for Phil, his opponent was Tiger Woods, who has been described as one of the most mentally tough performers in all of sport.

So the key point in this chapter is that it is important for you to have a balance of outcome and process orientations. In fact, my advice to you as a young athlete is that you should focus primarily on process. One reason that I say this is because an outcome orientation is something that seems to be ingrained in our society and in sport. American sportswriter Jerome Holtzman described this aptly when he said, "Losing is the great American sin." If you are reading this book, I'll bet that you already have a pretty strong outcome orientation and that you have some interest in winning at your sport. For this reason, I strongly encourage you to work on increasing your ability to focus on process because of the benefits that will follow.

The first benefit is that by focusing on process, you will be better able to develop as an athlete. As a young athlete who is in the midst of learning the game, you are honing your skills and becoming a technically sound player. Therefore, this is a time when it is vitally important to focus on process and to sometimes completely ignore outcome. For instance, perhaps you begin to experience some success in your sport and your coach asks you to learn something new. Imagine Henry is a baseball player and has been hitting well all season as a right-hander. Midway through the season, his coach asks him to begin switch-hitting. Henry begins to bat left-handed and is not able to swing the bat properly and can't make contact with the ball. How does he react to this? If he is focused purely on outcome, then he will not react well, because he will not be getting very many hits when he is learning this new skill. But if Henry is able to focus on process, then he will continue to hit as a left-hander in practice and in games and won't worry about outcomes like getting hits or getting on base. Ultimately, Henry will improve at his left-handed hitting and will enhance his development as a switch-hitter. This ability to hit right-handed or left-handed will then benefit Henry as he plays at higher levels, and by focusing on process, Henry will become a better player.

The second benefit is that by focusing on process rather than outcome, you free yourself up to face those competitors (in practice and in competition) who will challenge you and who will force you to improve. We've already talked about this effect a little, but let me give another example to further make this point. Janet Rayfield is the head coach for the University of Illinois women's soccer team and was a member of the U.S. Soccer Federation national staff. She tells a story of when she was coaching a team of young soccer players and had a parents' meeting at the start of the season. Coach Rayfield told the parents that she was going to try to arrange the season's schedule so that the team would win half of their games and lose half of their games. How do you think the parents responded to this statement? Were they happy to think that their children would be playing on a team that would win some and lose some? You probably aren't surprised to know that the parents were shocked and upset with what Coach Rayfield had said. They were upset because they wanted their children to play on a winning team, and this wasn't what Coach Rayfield was describing. Coach Rayfield had to explain to the parents that since their children were thirteen years old, the best season for them with regard to skill development would be a season in which they were challenged and only won half the time. She further explained that having a season in which they won every game was not important and would not help them to grow as players. Do you see how this works? Playing against a tough opponent with an uncertain outcome is the best way to improve your abilities both in terms of your skills and in terms of your ability to handle challenging competitions. If you only play against much weaker opponents, you may win the competitions, but you won't improve, and ultimately you won't have had the experiences necessary for you to reach your potential as an athlete.

Now, I recognize that it may be challenging for you to focus on process in the face of social and parental pressure to focus on winning. However, having a focus that balances a process orientation with an outcome orientation is incredibly important for young and older athletes alike. I challenge you to listen to the interviews of athletes in your sport and in other sports and see if you can figure out if they are outcome oriented or process oriented, or if they have a good balance between outcome and process. My bet is that the elite athletes will express that they focus on process more often than on outcome. Similarly, if you hear of an elite athlete who has dropped out of his or her sport due to burnout, my bet is that this athlete will say that the pressures of winning had taken the fun out of the game.

Changing your orientation to be focused more on process is similar to stopping negative self-talk (see Chapter 10). You should gain an awareness of what you focus on during games and even on what your friends, parents, and coaches focus on. For instance, after a game your parents didn't attend, what's the first question they ask you? Do they ask if you won or lost? My guess is that they do. But what questions would be better? It would be so much better if they asked how you played in the game or if you had fun in the game or if you felt like you improved in the game. These questions would demonstrate a focus on process, and if you answered that you played great, you had fun, and you felt like you improved from last week, then the outcome really isn't all that important. I like how the Australian swimmer Ian Thorpe put it: "For myself, losing is not coming in second. It's getting out of the water knowing you could have done better. For myself, I have won every race I've been in." Clearly, his emphasis is on process, not outcome, and he has felt successful at the conclusion of every race because he's always given his best effort.

The key for you, then, is to foster your focus on process but also to maintain an interest in outcome. Elite athletes demonstrate an ability to shift their focus between process and outcome in a way that benefits their development as athletes and as competitors. They are able to focus on process when they should and are also able to focus on outcome when they should. Natalie Coughlin won six medals in swimming at the Summer Olympics in 2008 but expressed that she was not happy with her initial performance and had to focus on process to improve. As she said, "My first swims were neither on par with my goals nor with my abilities. I could have mentally given up at that point. . . . Instead I focused more on my technique and relaxing away from the pool, and had faith that the training over the past several years cannot possibly go away overnight. With each swim my body was getting more and more comfortable racing again and my times improved." This ability to shift between a process orientation and an outcome orientation is a critical aspect of mental toughness and will be important for your development as an athlete.

## KEY POINTS

- People can be process oriented or outcome oriented or both.
- A process-oriented person focuses on the skills and techniques critical to performing well.
- An outcome-oriented person focuses on winning and outperforming others.
- A balanced person achieves success in sport by knowing how and when to focus on process and how and when to focus on outcome.

# Identify Your Balance between Outcome and Process

The Task and Ego Orientation Questionnaire was developed to assess process (task) and outcome (ego) orientations in athletes. Using a scale of 1–5, answer the following questions.

| 1 = strongly disagree  2 = disagree  3 = neutral  4 = agree  5 = strongly agree | | | | | |
|---|---|---|---|---|---|
| **I feel most successful in sport when . . .** | | | | | |
| 1. I am the only one who can perform the play or skill. | 1 | 2 | 3 | 4 | 5 |
| 2. I learn a new skill and it makes me want to practice more. | 1 | 2 | 3 | 4 | 5 |
| 3. I can do better than my friends. | 1 | 2 | 3 | 4 | 5 |
| 4. The others cannot do as well as me. | 1 | 2 | 3 | 4 | 5 |
| 5. I learn something that is fun to do. | 1 | 2 | 3 | 4 | 5 |
| 6. Others mess up *and* I do not. | 1 | 2 | 3 | 4 | 5 |
| 7. I learn a new skill by trying hard. | 1 | 2 | 3 | 4 | 5 |
| 8. I work really hard. | 1 | 2 | 3 | 4 | 5 |
| 9. I score the most points/goals/hits, etc. | 1 | 2 | 3 | 4 | 5 |
| 10. Something I learn makes me want to go practice more. | 1 | 2 | 3 | 4 | 5 |
| 11. I am the best. | 1 | 2 | 3 | 4 | 5 |
| 12. A skill I learn really feels right. | 1 | 2 | 3 | 4 | 5 |
| 13. I do my very best. | 1 | 2 | 3 | 4 | 5 |

*From J. L. Duda, "Relationship between Task and Ego Orientation and the Perceived Purpose of Sport among High School Athletes,"* Journal of Sport and Exercise Psychology *11 (1989): 318–35. Reprinted with permission.*

Add up the values for items 1, 3, 4, 6, 9, 11 and then divide by 6 →
   Outcome Score = _____.

Add up the values for items 2, 5, 7, 8, 10, 12, 13 and then divide by 7 →
   Process Score = _____.

To interpret these scores, we have to look at the average outcome and process scores that have been found in studies with athletes. The average is approximately 4.0 for process and approximately 2.8 for outcome.

If your process score is 4.0 or higher and if your outcome score is 2.8 or higher, you are reasonably high on both and probably have a good balance between the two. This is a sign that you have a good profile for success in sport. Continue working to maintain this balance and to learn when to focus on process and when to focus on outcome so that you continue to develop as an athlete and a competitor.

If you are low on either of these, then you should strive to increase your orientation in that regard.

If you are low on process (your score is less than 4.0), you should review your goal-setting sheet and your self-talk (see Chapter 10) to adjust your thinking to focus more on process. Identify when you are focusing on outcome and modify your thinking so that you are focused more on the process that is necessary to attain the outcome. As pointed out in this chapter, a focus on process is important because it affects your ability to improve at your sport.

If you are low on outcome (your score is less than 2.8), you are probably not currently focused on winning and outperforming others. I think that this is okay for a young athlete, but I recognize that the development of a stronger outcome orientation will be important as you move through the ranks in your sport. Because of the competitive nature of sport, there comes a time when outperforming others is the only way that you can define your success. For example, if you are trying out for the state select team, you will have to both perform your best and outperform the others who are competing for spots on this team. If you are hesitant to outperform the other competitors, this could be viewed negatively by coaches who value this characteristic in their athletes. Pretend that the coaches who are deciding who makes the varsity team have set up a series of one-versus-one competitions. You will be facing off individually against the other athletes. If you are not outcome oriented, you will not care specifically about beating your competitor. But this is all that counts in this particular situation. So if you focus only on your technique and performance, you may perform well and your technique may be flawless. But if you don't win the one-versus-one events, the coaches may not recognize your ability. If this describes you, then I encourage you to maintain your focus on process but to also recognize that in certain situations, focusing on beating your competition is appropriate. The others who have entered this competition are aware of this and will not take it personally if you beat them. You will be giving it your best if you focus on process but also strive to succeed in these situations.

# Attributions

"Attribution" is a term that sport psychologists use to describe how a performer explains the outcome of an event. In other words, an attribution is an explanation that is offered to describe why something came out the way it did. An attribution can be made either internally (to ourselves) or externally (said out loud to others or by others). When offering explanations for outcomes, people tend to be consistent in their use of a particular style of attributions. That is, they offer explanations that are either mostly positive or mostly negative. The attributions an athlete adopts can have serious effects on him or her down the road.

Unfortunately, many athletes use negative attributions to explain the outcomes of their own performances. That is, when athletes try to explain why they lost a game, they tend to use negative explanations. Even when they try to explain why they won a game, athletes often do not take full credit for their success, which is another example of a negative explanation. Negative attributions are problematic because if you use them on a regular basis, your self-confidence will decrease, your expectations for being successful in the future will be low, and your performance will ultimately suffer. On the other hand, if you use positive attributions to explain the outcomes of your sporting events, you will protect your self-confidence, you will have expectations that you will be successful in the future, and you will ultimately perform better in challenging situations. Let me give you some more descriptions and examples of negative and positive attributions so you can get a better sense of what these are and how they might affect you in the long run.

# Negative Attribution

## *Missed Opportunity*

There are two very common types of negative attributions. The first type we will call "Missed Opportunity." This is when you have a successful performance and you do not take credit for it. For example, imagine that you have just won a golf tournament and your friends come up to you and say, "Great tournament, how'd you do it?" Imagine that your response is "Well, I got very lucky on some shots. A couple of times I was in the sand and managed to get it back on the green. And my opponents really didn't play as well as they could." While this may seem like an appropriate and modest response, this attribution doesn't give *you* any credit for the outcome. Don't you think that part of your success is due to your preparation for the tournament, your game plan, your talent, your concentration, and your mental toughness? Instead of telling your friends the reasons why you were successful, you have explained your success in the tournament as being due to luck and to your opponents' poor play.

So imagine that the next question your friends ask you is "So, how do you expect to do in the next tournament?" What would you say? Since you just said that you only won this tournament because you got lucky and your opponents played poorly, your response to this second question would have to be "I don't know what will happen in the next tournament. Hopefully my opponents will continue to play poorly and I'll get lucky again." Clearly, because you did not take credit for your success and explained your victory as being due to things that are not in your control (luck and opponents' poor play), your expectations for the next tournament are uncertain. In other words, because you cannot control how your opponents will play and you certainly cannot control luck, there is no way that you can know what to expect in the next competition. In addition to resulting in uncertainty about the next competition, your explanation also represents a Missed Opportunity because you have let an opportunity for confidence building (see Chapter 16) slip away. Remember, YOU WON THE TOURNAMENT! After winning a tournament, you should make an attribution that will contribute to your confidence in your ability to play well and that will suggest that future successes are likely and are in your control.

# Positive Attribution

## *Taking Credit*

Given the example above, a more positive attribution would be to use a "Taking Credit" explanation. A Taking Credit explanation for winning the tournament would be "I prepared well and practiced hard for this tournament. I gave 100% effort for the entire round. And when I did get into the sand, I really focused and was able to get myself out of trouble." Although this is still a very modest response, the explanation allows you to take credit as the one who made it happen. By making a positive Taking Credit attribution like this, your self-confidence should increase because the explanation itself says that you won the tournament because you deserved and earned it. The Taking Credit attribution also results in an expectation that you can be successful in the future because you have stated that you won this tournament because of things that are in your control and that don't rely on others or on luck. So when your friends ask, "So, how do you expect to do in the next tournament?" your answer can be "I expect to do well in the next tournament, too, because I will continue to practice hard and give 100% effort in my competitions."

# Negative Attribution

## *Taking the Blame*

The second type of negative attribution that is especially common in team sports is called "Taking the Blame." A Taking the Blame attribution is when you take all of the blame for an unsuccessful performance. For example, imagine your team has just lost a game and you think to yourself, "I lost the game for us. The player I was defending scored the game-winner. I'm a poor defender." This type of attribution is incredibly common but is both inaccurate and hurtful to your self-confidence and expectations for the future. This explanation is inaccurate because it does not reflect reality. In any game, no matter what type of mistake you might have made, the outcome depends on an infinite number of events; no single mistake (or even a series of mistakes) could ever fully explain it. If you are discussing a basketball game, then it is not likely that your team had zero opportunities to score and lost 2-0 when the

By using a Taking Credit attribution following a competition, you bolster your confidence and your expectation that you will perform well at the next competition.

only basket was scored by your defensive assignment. Clearly, in basketball or any team sport, there are many opportunities to score and many opportunities to play defense, and all of those contribute to the final score. No matter what happens in the final seconds, you cannot deny that the end result is based on the total number of points scored by each team, and this is determined by multiple scoring and multiple defending opportunities. Even if you were playing a game like soccer where there are usually very few scoring opportunities, a loss is never the fault of any single player. Imagine that your team lost 1-0 after your defensive assignment scored the lone goal. This loss still cannot be your fault alone because there were an infinite number of things that happened between the starting whistle and the game-over whistle that contributed to your team's loss. There were passes completed and passes not completed, fouls called, defensive decisions made, offensive opportunities lost, and shots taken and not taken. All of these events, actions, and decisions determined the final outcome of the game. What happened on any single scoring opportunity cannot by itself explain the final score.

Besides being inaccurate, this Taking the Blame attribution harms your self-confidence and lowers your expectations for how well you will perform in the future. In other words, because your attribution includes the explanation that you are "a poor defender"—a description of a relatively permanent aspect of your game—you will remain a poor defender in your mind when you play next week, which will affect how you play in the game. Thus, by fully taking the blame for the outcome of this event and describing yourself as a poor defender, your explanation for the outcome of this game has implications for your expectations and performance in the next game.

## Positive Attribution

### *Poor Process*

A more positive way to interpret the outcome just described would be to make a "Poor Process" attribution. Continuing with the basketball example, you might have said, "My player scored the game-winner because I made a mistake on defense. I will have to focus on my defense in the future, but I am happy with my overall performance and effort in the game." Here you are focusing an attribution on process rather than on outcome (see Chapter 8). You'll notice that there is nothing wrong with admitting that you made a mistake in the game. This statement may be a realistic and honest explanation of what happened and is perfectly okay, because there is no athlete in the world who can say that he or she has never made a mistake in competition. In fact, taking responsibility for mistakes and using them to help you to become a better player are keys to mental toughness. I love this quote by Michael Jordan: "I've missed more than 9,000 shots in my career. I've lost almost 300 games. Twenty-six times, I've been trusted to take the game winning shot and missed. I've failed over and over and over again in my life. And that is why I succeed." The key to turning mistakes into success is learning from them and attributing them to aspects of your game that are in your control, like your effort and your preparation for the game.

Using a Poor Process attribution is a positive style of attributing because the statement focuses on something that is in your control. That is, rather than thinking, "I'm a poor defender," you thought, "I made a mistake on defense"; making this simple switch in your thinking suggests room for improvement before the next competition. If you focus more on defense in upcoming practices and games to try to avoid making this same type of mistake again, you will improve your overall game. You can see, too, that this type of attribution does not have a negative effect on self-confidence but, rather, suggests that in future similar situations, you can succeed because you control your behavior and defensive skills through your efforts to improve these parts of your game.

The use of positive attributions contributes to mental toughness. By taking credit for our successes and by realistically explaining our failures, we protect our self-confidence and ensure that we have expectations for success in future competitions. This is not to say that you should never accept responsibility for a poor performance. As mentioned, it is okay to accept a reasonable and realistic share of the responsibility for the outcome of a sporting event. But it is critically important that you protect your self-confidence by attributing losses to things that you can improve upon and to things that are not a part of you, and by attributing successes to things that you can control and that are a part of you. To clarify this last part about attributions, imagine that you have suffered a series of losses and that you attribute each of these losses to poor ability (as in "I am not a good defender"). Since your ability as a defender is a part of you and is not changeable in the short term, you are really saying that you are "no good at defense" and that you should not expect to be successful in the future. This is not a mentally tough way of thinking because this sets you up to expect failure in the future and, in some ways, allows you to shirk responsibility for improving your defensive performance. In other words, saying "I'm not a good defender" can be viewed as a cop-out that mentally allows you to *not* put in the necessary effort to improve your defending abilities.

In contrast, the mentally tough athlete explains his or her contribution to a loss as being due to controllable aspects of performance, such as a lack of focus and a need to practice more at defense. By making

By attributing an unsuccessful performance to Poor Process, you can focus on improving a weakness and will have positive expectations for future competitions.

these types of positive attributions even in the face of a series of losses, the mentally tough athlete protects his or her self-confidence and focuses on improving for future competitions. This allows the mentally tough athlete to take responsibility for improving and to continue developing as a player.

• Attributions are explanations we offer for the outcomes of events.

• Many people only use negative attributions, which result in low self-confidence, low expectations for future success, and poor performance.

• It is important to use positive attributions for our wins and losses in sport. Positive attributions result in high self-confidence, high expectations for future success, and good performance.

• Here are some examples of positive attributions for wins:

  ○ My game plan was effective and I executed it well.

  ○ I trained hard and I played well today.

  ○ I am a skilled athlete and I gave 100% effort.

  ○ I have been working hard to perform well in this event.

• Here are some examples of positive attributions for losses:

  ○ My game plan could have been better.

  ○ I was not fit enough for the competition.

  ○ I did not play well today.

  ○ I did not give 100% effort.

  ○ I lost my focus toward the end of the competition.

# Identify the Attributions You Used to Explain Recent Outcomes

Think of a recent competition in which you were successful. Write down some of the reasons for your success. Look carefully at the reasons you have written down. Are these positive attributions? Make sure that you do not have explanations that result in a Missed Opportunity. If you find a negative explanation, rewrite it to be positive. Also, are you Taking Credit for your success? If not, add an extra explanation that gives yourself credit for your success.

*Description of Successful Competition*

_____

_____

|  | POSITIVE OR NEGATIVE |
| REASONS FOR MY SUCCESS | ATTRIBUTION? |
| --- | --- |
| 1. _____ | _____ |
| 2. _____ | _____ |
| 3. _____ | _____ |
| 4. _____ | _____ |
| 5. _____ | _____ |

**CORRECTED ATTRIBUTION**

| # . _____ | _____ |
| --- | --- |
| # . _____ | _____ |

Think of a recent competition in which you think you were not successful. Write down some of the reasons for your lack of success. Look carefully at the reasons you have written down. Are these reasons positive? Do you focus on Poor Process as an explanation of your lack of success? Are you Taking the Blame for outcomes that were not totally in your control? Be sure that none of your explanations are negative. If you identify a negative attribution, rewrite it to be positive.

### Description of Unsuccessful Competition

_____

_____

| REASONS FOR MY LACK OF SUCCESS | POSITIVE OR NEGATIVE ATTRIBUTION? |
|---|---|
| 1. _____ | _____ |
| 2. _____ | _____ |
| 3. _____ | _____ |
| 4. _____ | _____ |
| 5. _____ | _____ |

**CORRECTED ATTRIBUTION**

| # . _____ | _____ |
|---|---|
| # . _____ | _____ |

In future competitions, strive to use positive attributions. Applaud yourself for your successes. Don't overly criticize your abilities when you are not successful. In all cases, focus on process and on aspects of your game that are in your control. As you work to develop mental toughness, you should notice that your attributions become increasingly more positive and that you no longer have to correct any negative attributions. Once you are using only positive attributions, you will begin to experience improvements in your confidence and in your expectations for future success. This is a key to mental toughness.

# 10

# Self-Talk

As mentioned in the preceding chapter, attributions can be made either internally or externally. When attributions are made internally, they are a form of self-talk. Self-talk is defined as the internal dialogue that takes place inside your own head. It is the internal conversation that you have with yourself. Like attributions, self-talk can be either positive or negative. Unfortunately, many people have very negative self-talk, which they practice frequently. In fact, some people have such frequent negative self-talk that they are their own worst critics and even their own worst enemies.

## Negative Self-Talk

### Mean Self-Talk

Negative self-talk comes in two major forms. The first form is what I will call Mean Self-Talk. This negative self-talk is probably the worst kind because it is just flat out mean and hurtful. Examples of Mean Self-Talk are saying to yourself, "I suck," "I stink," or "I can't believe I did something so stupid." Obviously, these are not nice things to say, and you would probably not say them out loud to anyone else, nor would you want anyone else to say these things to you. In fact, if your friends said these things to you on a regular basis, you would probably not stay friends for very long. But despite the fact that you wouldn't tell your friends "You suck" or "You're stupid," you might say these mean things to yourself all the time. Think about how hearing these types of statements makes you feel. Imagine hearing these types of negative phrases all the time. Hearing such comments repeatedly would make you feel terrible about yourself and would have a negative effect on your self-confidence, your happiness, and ultimately your performance. So to reach your performance potential, you must identify any Mean Self-Talk that you are using, eliminate it, and replace it with more positive forms of self-talk.

## Negative Predictions

The second form of negative self-talk is Negative Predictions. For example, an athlete might say internally, "I hate these types of shots; I never make these types of shots" or "I haven't stuck this landing yet." The trouble with these internal statements is that they frequently create reality. Notice that I said they frequently "create" reality rather than that they "reflect" reality. If we keep saying to ourselves over and over that we are going to miss a particular shot, should we be surprised when we do miss that shot? And then, after missing that shot, we have just confirmed what we think we already knew. That is, we thought we would miss the shot and we did miss the shot and so we must have been right in thinking that we would miss the shot. Then, since we were right, we feel justified in making these Negative Predictions again. Do you see how this can become a vicious cycle?

Again, the issue is that a Negative Prediction can become a powerful self-fulfilling prophecy. In other words, if you tell me before taking a shot that you think you are going to miss it, then I would be willing to bet $10 that you will miss the shot. I fully believe that your self-talk has an impact on the outcome of the shot. Although your practice and your other preparations for performance might have been perfect, this simple Negative Prediction can be an incredibly powerful way to erase a lot of hard work. You must learn to replace any Negative Predictions with Positive Predictions—they, too, result in a self-fulfilling prophecy, but you are predicting a positive outcome.

Imagine that you are playing golf and you are attempting to make a putt with about twelve feet of green between the ball and the hole. You have one of two options as you're lining up to take the shot. You can say, "I hate putts that are this distance. I know I should make this, but it's just a little too far. I always miss this shot. I need to try not to flinch." Or you can say, "I know I've missed putts like this before, but I'm confident today that I'll make this putt. I've got it lined up well and I'm sure I'm going to sink this. I need to use a smooth stroke." Which one of these forms of self-talk do you think will result in a made putt? Which one will result in a missed putt? It's a simple relationship and an important key to being a mentally tough athlete and a consistent performer. Use

Negative predictions that you make in your self-talk can create reality, and then the outcome reinforces your negative prediction.

Positive Predictions and create a positive reality for yourself! Although doubt may creep in, use positive self-talk to increase your confidence, master your emotions, and create a sense of readiness.

## Thought-Stopping

To master your self-talk, you must learn to eliminate negative self-talk and replace it with more positive forms. You can do this through a process called thought-stopping. The first step in the process of thought-stopping is to gain an awareness of your self-talk. Start listening to yourself to hear what you are saying inside your head. For example, if you have just missed the first of two free throws, you may hear yourself combining Mean Self-Talk and Negative Predictions by saying, "I suck. I never make free throws. I knew I'd miss that last free throw and I'll probably miss this one, too. I always hit the front of the rim." When you hear yourself starting on this track, you should use thought-stopping to stop the negatives and shift to positives. You should gently reprimand yourself by saying, "Wait. That's negative self-talk. I should not be thinking like this." Take a deep breath or two and consciously change your self-talk to something like "Okay, I missed that free-throw, but it's behind me now and out of my control. What I can control is how I approach this next free throw. I've just got to focus on the follow-through." In your head, you may then say "Just follow through" as you are stroking the ball toward the basket. If you practice this sequence of steps frequently, you will eventually learn to completely avoid negative self-talk, and more positive self-talk will become automatic. When you have reached this stage, thought-stopping is no longer necessary because you have become a mentally tough athlete who uses positive self-talk to prepare for and react to events in your sport. As you master the art of using positive self-talk, you can also include more affirming types of statements. Begin to incorporate statements into your self-talk that are self-promoting, like "My practices have been great. I am well-prepared and expect to have one of the best performances here today."

## Positive Self-Talk

Obviously, practicing positive self-talk will not by itself make you a successful performer. You must combine positive self-talk with all of the other aspects of your preparation and training. If you are prepared physically and have practiced your performance to perfection, then one additional piece to the puzzle is using positive self-talk to increase your confidence and create a positive reality. You should practice using positive self-talk much like you practice physically for your sport. Combine positive self-talk with your performances so that positive self-talk becomes an automatic part of your competitive performances. In fact, you should make positive self-talk a part of your pre-performance routines (see Chapter 13).

In addition to using positive self-talk during practices and in competition, you must also become skilled at using positive self-talk even during difficult times. You will make mistakes in competitions. You may even make huge mistakes. For example, in the women's World Cup in soccer in 1999 the U.S. women's team was playing against the German women's team to try to advance to the semifinals. In the early minutes of the game, Brandy Chastain was playing defense, and she and goalie Brianna Scurry miscommunicated, which resulted in Brandy accidentally heading the ball into the U.S. goal right past Brianna. Can you imagine? The biggest tournament in the world and you've just scored an "own goal" that has put the other team ahead 1-0? This is probably the worst mistake imaginable in soccer! What would you say to yourself if you had done this? What do you think Brandy was saying to herself? Brandy might have said terrible things to herself in response to this mistake. But what if she didn't say those negative things? What if she said positive things instead? Do you think that might influence what happened next in terms of her own play and in terms of the game?

Read the possibilities below and think about how these two different types of self-talk would affect Brandy differently.

*Mean Self-Talk and Negative Predictions*: "I can't believe I just did that. What an idiot! I shouldn't even be out here. What was I thinking? I've put my team behind and now we're going to lose the game and won't make it to the semifinals. I hope the ball doesn't come my way again because now I'm such a basket case that I'll probably mess up again."

*Positive Self-Talk*: "Okay, I made a mistake. Okay, I made a big mistake. But, that mistake is in the past and it's out of my control. I am going to have to work hard and focus on things that I can control so that I can make a positive difference in this game. I'm going to step up my work rate and get the ball back for my team so we can get an opportunity to score."

In this game, Brandy must have used positive self-talk. Do you know

By saying positive, confident things to yourself,
you increase your likelihood for success.

how I know? If Brandy's self-talk had included Mean Self-Talk and Negative Predictions, how do you think she would have played? Do you think
the coach and her teammates would have noticed if she wasn't playing well? If Brandy had used negative self-talk, her coach and teammates would have seen her performance disintegrate and she would
have been substituted out of the game. But Brandy's mental toughness
was evidenced by the fact that she recovered and played well from that
point forward. In fact, she came back so strongly following this mistake
that she was kept in the game, played solid defense for the remainder of
the game, and ultimately ended up scoring a goal for the United States
toward the end of the game.

While it is definitely better to use positive self-talk than to use negative self-talk, it is important to realize that your positive self-talk should be based in reality. That is, you should not use unrealistic self-talk even if it is very positive. For example, you should not say to yourself, "I am the greatest player who ever lived." Unrealistic self-talk will not result in a sudden bestowment of talent that you have not worked for. In fact, if your self-talk is unrealistic and if you haven't put in the preparations to give yourself the opportunity to be successful, then it is likely to be harmful. For instance, if you tell yourself, "I am the greatest player who ever lived," you give yourself a message that you do not need to practice and that you do not need to focus on your performance, and poor performance will likely be the result. After only a few poor performances, you would realize that your self-talk is wildly inaccurate, and you might have a real crisis in your confidence.

You should, however, use realistic positive self-talk on a regular basis and say things such as "I have been training hard, I have put in the proper preparation, and I am the best I can be today." You should have positive conversations like this with yourself on a regular basis, and you should ensure that these conversations are grounded in reality by putting in the hard work necessary to make the statements true. By using positive self-talk frequently, not only will you improve your performance, but you will also be a happier person because you hear nice things in your head instead of mean things.

## KEY POINTS

- What we say to ourselves in our heads is called self-talk.
- Negative self-talk hurts our confidence and can create a negative reality.
- Positive self-talk helps our self-confidence and creates a positive reality.
- Gain an awareness of your self-talk. Use thought-stopping techniques to identify negative self-talk and replace it with positive self-talk.
- Increase your positive self-talk as much as possible and keep it realistic. This will boost your self-confidence and help you to create a positive reality.

# What Should I Be Saying to Myself?

1. Terry is a talented gymnast who is about to perform his most difficult and challenging routine. What should Terry say to himself before he performs?

2. Kari is a young golfer who has just hit three bad tee shots in a row. She is stepping up to the tee to take her shot. The other golfers in her group have just hit very nice balls right down the fairway. What should Kari say to herself as she approaches the ball.

3. Carolyn is a swimmer who competes in both individual and team events for her college team. She was expected to win her last individual event but came in a disappointing fourth place. Her relay team is just getting ready for their event, what should she say to herself?

4. Imagine that you are about to do something challenging in your sport (like take a really important shot, complete a difficult move, or perform against a challenging competitor). What should you say to yourself as you approach this event?

# Controlling the Controllables

This chapter goes hand in hand with the preceding chapter on self-talk. Thus far in this book, I have mentioned a few times that an important part of mental toughness is focusing only on those aspects of your game that are in your control and recognizing that you cannot control everything in any situation. The fact is, in many situations you can only control a relatively small number of the variables that ultimately influence the outcome. In other words, in any given situation there are a huge number of variables that will contribute to the final outcome, and most of these variables are completely out of your control. Let me give you an example from the sport of baseball that illustrates what I mean.

Max pitches for his high school baseball team and has done absolutely everything in his power to prepare for the state championship game. Max is fit, has a good game plan, has practiced until his technical skills are sound, has worked hard with his catcher and the pitching coach to improve his tactical abilities and knowledge of the game, and has done the proper pre-game preparations. The game begins, and Max is playing well. His team is ahead 2-0 in the fifth inning. Suddenly, the clouds that have been present all morning seem to gather strength, and rain begins to pour down. After a brief conference, the umpires decide that the game will have to be delayed until the rain lets up. All of the players are sent to the dugouts to wait it out. So how does Max deal with this? How does he cope with a sudden delay in the game when he had been pitching extremely well and his team was ahead? How does he handle the fact that no one can predict when they might get back out on the field to continue the game?

Imagine that Max focuses his concentration and thoughts on the weather and has a running internal conversation (self-talk) that goes

By keeping his focus on things that are within his control, Max will be ready to go when the rain stops and the game resumes.

something like this: "I can't believe there has been a rain delay. I was playing great. Now I'm going to get cold and tight and will have to warm up all over again. The umpires are idiots. We should be playing through this. There isn't any lightning, we should just keep playing. I know I won't be ready if we wait too much longer. This rain has got to stop!" If Max uses this self-talk, how do you think he will pitch when the umpire says, "Play ball"? Max has chosen to focus on things he cannot control. Obviously, the weather, the decisions of the umpires, and the speed at which the field will dry are not under his control. To focus on these things will not help Max cope with this unexpected turn of events; rather, it will result in Max being distracted and failing to perform at his best when the game resumes.

So what should Max be saying to himself? What should his self-talk sound like during this break in play? If Max is mentally tough, he will use this unexpected rain delay to focus on things that he can control and to continue his preparations for competition. He will spend the time during the rain delay mentally imagining his continued good performance, keeping warm, stretching, and talking strategy with the pitching coach. He will prepare for the next few batters he will be facing. He will use his relaxation skills to keep his energy at the appropriate level. He will interact with his teammates to help them stay focused and ready to play. If Max is mentally tough, then he will be able to step back onto the pitcher's mound as soon as play resumes, and he will demonstrate his mental toughness and confidence by quickly continuing his good performance.

Learning to focus your energy on things that are within your control is a mental skill that most top-level athletes have. After particularly tough competitions, you will frequently hear top-level athletes say that they focused on things that were in their control and not on things that were out of their control. Carl Lewis, winner of nine Olympic gold medals in track and field, described this well when he said, "My thoughts before a big race are usually pretty simple. I tell myself: Get out of the blocks, run your race, stay relaxed. If you run your race, you'll win.... Channel your energy. Focus." To learn to focus on the controllables requires gaining an awareness of the thoughts that you have. Again, you should learn to pay close attention to your self-talk. Identify your thoughts and monitor your internal conversation to see if you are focusing on things that are in your control or if you are focusing on things that are out of your control (see sidebar for examples). If you notice that you are focusing on things that are out of your control, you must work to shift your focus to things that you can control.

## Thought-Stopping

The most effective tool for shifting your focus from things that are out of your control to things that are in your control is thought-stopping (see Chapter 10). The first step in the process of thought-stopping is to

# Examples of controllable variables and of uncontrollable variables

| Controllable Variables | Uncontrollable Variables |
|---|---|
| Your fitness level | An injury |
| Your game plan | The weather |
| Your effort level | A poor call by an official |
| Your intensity | An incredible play/shot/performance |
| Your self-talk | by an opponent |
| Your pre-game preparation | Comments from the fans/your opponent |
| Your concentration level | A bad bounce |
| Execution of technique | A missed scoring opportunity |

gain an awareness of what you are saying to yourself in your internal dialogue and of what you are saying to others. When you recognize that you are focusing on things that are out of your control, simply say to yourself, "Stop, that is not in your control," and then change your focus to aspects of the game that are in your control. When you are just beginning to learn this way of thinking, you may have to monitor your thoughts closely, and you may have to force yourself to make this change in your thought patterns. But as you continue to practice focusing on the aspects of the game that are under your control, you will begin to find that this way of thinking will become more automatic for you. Then, by changing your focus to aspects of the game that are under your control, you will start to see a change in your performance. Also, by focusing on controllable variables that you can adjust immediately, you will keep your energies directed where they should be in the competition. By identifying aspects of your performance that are in your control and focusing energy on these aspects, you can increase your ability to execute.

Mia Hamm, a member of the U.S. women's soccer team for eighteen years and winner of two World Cups and two Olympic medals, described this well when she said, "As players, when we are having a bad day, we tend to think in melodramatic terms, that we've lost it, that everything's gone wrong, but usually all you have to do is correct one small element of your game and everything else will fall into place." Clearly, Mia is expressing that by focusing on an aspect of your game that is within your control, you can improve your performance.

Let me provide another example of the importance of focusing on controllable aspects of your game as opposed to allowing a focus on uncontrollable aspects to dominate. Tennis provides a great opportunity to literally *see* whether or not athletes are mentally tough because of the obvious display of emotions on the faces and in the behaviors of the athletes. During competition, Serena Williams is one of the most mentally tough athletes you will ever see. However, I have seen Serena play several matches in which she has stepped onto the tennis court appearing to be somewhat unprepared mentally for the event (something she could certainly improve with her pre-game routine) and not in her best match-fitness shape (something she could improve with her training program). In fact, she has frequently begun a match playing below her potential and making mistakes that are not typical for her. She then falls behind and must improve her play to stay in the match (and the tournament). Almost without fail, Serena does just that. And you can tell that she makes the switch by focusing on the things in the match that she can control. Once behind, she certainly cannot control the score and she also cannot control her opponent's level of play. But she can focus her energies on controlling the important aspects of her game, and that is exactly what she does. You will see on her face a strengthened concentration, a focus on serving well, a focus on hitting solid groundstrokes, a focus on footwork and moving well to prepare for the ball, and a focus on placing the ball accurately and not forcing the play. Time and time again, when Serena makes this switch and gathers herself to focus on these controllable aspects of her game, the match swings around, and frequently Serena comes from behind to win. As you continue to develop your own mental toughness, use positive self-talk to help you maintain your focus on aspects of your performance that are under your control. When you focus on these controllable variables, the consistency of your performance will increase and your level of performance will improve.

• Mentally tough athletes are able to focus their concentration on aspects of the competition that are within their control and do not waste their energies focusing on things that are out of their control.

• Gain awareness of both your internal and your external conversations. If you notice that these conversations focus on things that are out of your control, use thought-stopping to stop the conversation and change the focus to controllable variables.

• By focusing on aspects of the competition that are in your control, you contribute to your ability to perform at your potential on a consistent basis.

# Change Your Focus from Uncontrollables to Controllables

The statements below illustrate examples of conversations that focus on uncontrollable variables. Rewrite these statements so that they focus on controllable variables instead.

1. "I can't believe I missed that last shot. I wish I'd made that shot. That shot could have made the difference."

2. "I have a headache that won't quit. My head is pounding. I took something a few minutes ago, but I don't think it will help for at least another twenty minutes or so."

3. "Coach didn't start me in this game. He said I'd go in as a substitute, but I just can't believe he didn't start me. I wonder why he's mad at me. I wish I hadn't asked my parents to come."

4. "The wind today is unbelievable. How can we be expected to compete under these conditions. I never perform well when it's windy like this."

5. Write a sentence or two that you've said either internally or externally and that expresses a misplaced focus on uncontrollable variables.

Correct your sentence to illustrate a focus on controllable variables.

# Energy Management

Have you ever noticed when you watch sporting events that some athletes seem to perform better when they're excited and pumped up and others perform better when they appear to be calm and relaxed? This is true for all of us. Whether you are calm and relaxed or excited and pumped up affects your performance. You've probably also noticed that your energy level changes from day to day. Some days you feel really energized and ready to go, and other times you feel more passive and laid back. Your sport performance may also be uneven. Some days you make very few mistakes, feel ready for anything, and perform beautifully, yet other days you make a lot of mistakes, feel unable to anticipate what's going to happen next, and perform poorly. A variable that contributes to this inconsistency in performance is your energy level. Identifying the level of energy that is ideal for you is a key to performing your best on a consistent basis.

So what exactly do we mean by energy level? Your energy level is your overall amount of excitement or stimulation. At any given time, your energy level can be anywhere between really low (like when you are sleepy or drowsy) or really high (like when you are bouncing off the walls with excitement). Energy levels are important because they can be a key factor in determining how well you perform. If your energy is at the perfect level for you, then your performance will be good. But if you are too excited or too calm, then your performance will suffer. So you must identify the amount of energy that is right for you to have your best performance, and then you need to learn energy management skills that will help you attain this level of energy on a regular basis. This will result in consistently good performance.

## How Energy Levels Affect Performance

Your level of energy affects your mental and physical abilities, which, in turn, affect performance. In terms of mental abilities, your energy level has an impact on the number and type of cues that you are able to pay attention to during performance. Cues are anything in the environment that you can see or think about. Cues can be either relevant to your performance (like knowing the score) or not relevant to your performance (like wishing that your teacher would cancel tomorrow's exam).

Energy levels have an important impact on the number and types of cues that you pay attention to because your energy influences the width of your attention. As your energy increases from low to high, your attentional width moves from being very wide to being very narrow (see fig. 12.1). Let's look at the relationship between energy, attentional width, and performance at three levels (low, high, and "just right"). When your energy is low, your attentional width is so wide that you pay attention to cues that are not important for you to perform well. In other words, instead of focusing only on cues that are important for performance, you also focus on cues that distract you from your performance, like wondering what you're having for dinner tonight, wishing you didn't have so much homework, and thinking about a recent episode of your favorite television show. When your energy is high, your attentional width is too narrow, and you miss some of the necessary cues for performance. In other words, your energy is so high that you're not able to focus on *all* of the factors that are critical for performance. But when your energy is just right, your attentional width is perfect, and you are able to attend to the relevant cues for performance and to ignore the unimportant cues. Your goal is to strive to achieve your "just right" level of energy, since you will perform best when you have an ideal attentional width.

As an example of these low, high, and just right energy states and how they affect attention and performance, imagine three basketball players named Liz, Helen, and Payton. These players are performing at very different levels of energy, which has a direct impact on their performance.

Liz is not very excited about tonight's game. As a result, her energy is too low, and her attentional width is too wide. Therefore, Liz ends up paying attention to cues that are both important and unimportant for the game. Liz is aware of much of the information that she needs to perform well. She knows the defensive pattern of the other team, she

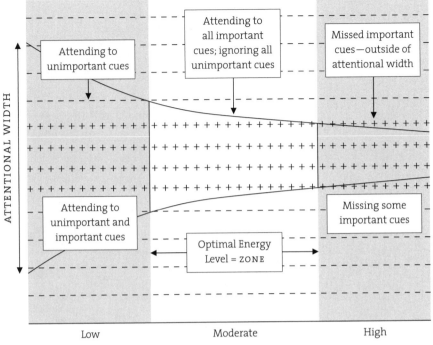

ATTENTIONAL WIDTH

Attending to
unimportant cues

Attending to
all important
cues; ignoring all
unimportant cues

Missed important
cues—outside of
attentional width

+ + + + + + + + + + + + + + + + + + + + + + + + + + + + + + + + + + + + + +
+ + + + + + + + + + + + + + + + + + + + + + + + + + + + + + + + + + + + + +
+ + + + + + + + + + + + + + + + + + + + + + + + + + + + + + + + + + + + + +
+ + + + + + + + + + + + + + + + + + + + + + + + + + + + + + + + + + + + + +

Attending to
unimportant and
important cues

Missing some
important cues

Optimal Energy
Level = ZONE

Low                    Moderate                    High

YOUR ENERGY LEVEL

FIGURE 12.1. Your energy level ranges from low to high and affects your attentional width. At low levels of energy, your attention is too broad, and you attend to both unimportant and important cues. At high levels of energy, your attention is too narrow, and you miss important cues. When you are in your zone, you are able to attend to all of the important cues and to ignore the unimportant cues. (Based on D. M. Landers, "The Arousal-Performance Relationship Revisited," *Research Quarterly for Exercise and Sport* 51 [1980]: 82.)

knows the offensive play that her team has called, and she knows her role in the play. This is good because this information is obviously important for her to execute the play. But Liz is also thinking about her parents sitting up in the stands, wondering where her little brother went since he's not up there with them right now, and thinking about talking to her friends after the game. Clearly, this information will distract Liz, hurting her concentration and keeping her from performing her best. So because Liz's energy is too low, she is focused on cues in the environment that are not relevant to the game of basketball, and as a result, Liz's performance will suffer.

When your energy level is too low, like Liz's, you pay attention to things that are distracting, and this has a negative effect on your performance.

Helen is extremely excited about the game and is very fired up to play, but her energy is too high. As a result, Helen's attentional width is too narrow. Helen, therefore, pays attention to some of the cues that are important for the game but also misses some key information needed for her to perform well. Helen is not thinking about the people in the

When your energy level is too high, like Helen's, you are not aware of everything that's important for you to perform well.

stands or what she's going to have for dinner. Instead, Helen is focused only on the basketball itself. But Helen also does not know what offensive play has been called or what defensive pattern the other team is playing. Helen is so highly energized that she is not paying attention to important aspects of the game that would help her to perform well. Because of her narrow focus and her lack of awareness, Helen is likely to make a mistake such as passing the ball to the other team, and she will not be able to perform at her best until she gets her energy to a more moderate level.

Payton has come to the game with an ideal level of energy. She's excited to play but has a calmness about her own performance that results in an ideal level of energy that is perfect for her. She is aware of the important cues and information for performance but is also blocking out information and cues that are not important for the game. Payton is aware of the defensive pattern of the other team, knows the offensive play her team has called, and knows her role in the execution of the

When your energy level is perfect for you, like Payton's, you are able to block out distractions and pay attention to the aspects of the game that are important—and you perform at your best!

play. She is not missing anything important to play well. Payton ignores things that would detract from her performance. Payton's parents are in the stands, but she is not thinking about them and doesn't even realize that her cousin Sophie came, too. Because Payton has an ideal level of energy, her attentional width is at the optimal level, and she will be able to perform at her best.

To play at your best on a regular basis, you need to learn what level of energy helps you to perform the best, and then you must master energy management techniques that will enable you to achieve this level of energy before competition.

## Differences in the Optimal Level of Energy

One interesting thing about energy levels is that the right level for optimal performance will not be the same for everybody. The best energy level for you may not be the same as that for your teammate. You may play best when you are really pumped up, when your heart is pounding, and when your excitement level is high. But your teammate may play best when he or she is at a lower level of energy and appears to be relatively calm and relaxed. Think about the big differences in the energy levels displayed by professional football players. Some players, such as Dallas Cowboys receiver Terrell Owens, act very excited and jump around on the sidelines. Other players, however, such as Indianapolis Colts receiver Marvin Harrison, stay very calm and even-keeled during the competition. If these players are using good energy management skills so that they are at the optimal energy level for them, they will perform well even though their levels of energy are very different.

The optimal level of energy for performance will also differ between sports. For example, in track and field events, performance may generally be better with relatively high levels of energy. Athletes who come to track and field competitions with a high level of energy and excitement are likely to perform better than athletes who cannot get as energized. On the other hand, performance in golf will generally be better with a relatively low level of energy. Golfers who are able to keep their energy low in high-pressure situations are likely to perform better than golfers whose hearts are pounding and who are overly excited during those same situations. This difference between sports is largely related to the impact of energy levels on physical abilities. Sports that require powerful movements performed by large muscle groups (like track, where the goal is to pump your legs as fast as you can) benefit from high energy. Sports that require smaller movements performed with accuracy as a goal (like golf, where you must put the right pace on the ball as you putt it toward the hole) benefit from low energy. In general, activities that benefit from a higher level of energy are those that require speed, strength, and the use of large muscle groups (like sprinting, blocking, putting the shot, throwing the javelin, lifting weights, and wrestling). Alternatively, activities that benefit from a lower level of energy are those that require finesse, accuracy, and the use of few or smaller muscle groups (like putting in golf, shooting free throws, marksmanship, and archery).

If you have ever watched the skiing biathlon in the winter Olympics, however, you've seen an event that specifically challenges the relationship between energy levels and performance. In the biathlon, skiers race around a cross-county course as quickly and powerfully as they can. The race is broken up by shooting events that require the athletes to either stand or lie down to shoot five targets with a rifle. If they miss any of the targets, extra time or distance is added to their race performance. The racers who are the most successful are those who are best able to manage their energy levels. They must be energized and highly aroused to race as quickly as they can around the cross-country course, but when it is time to shoot, they must be able to quickly control their energy so that they can shoot with accuracy.

As a last note about energy, even within the same sport, players at different positions may require different levels of energy for optimal performance; even different skills within the same sport may require different levels of energy. In football, for example, the optimal energy level for a quarterback is likely to be lower than the optimal energy level for a defensive end. When the quarterback is trying to scan the field for an open receiver, a lower level of energy may be ideal to allow for attention to a broad range of cues for performance. The quarterback must pay attention to the movement patterns of the entire defensive team, has to be aware of the patterns being run by the wide receivers, needs to know where the first-down line is, and must time the pass to meet the end of the receiver's run. The defensive end, on the other hand, may need a higher level of energy to have the strength, speed, and power to get past the blockers and may not need to focus on as many cues for performance. However, the situation can change quickly if the defensive end gets around the blockers and the quarterback needs to tuck the ball and run. Then the quarterback had better have a higher level of energy so that he can make a hasty escape!

For examples of how different skills within the same sport might require different levels of energy, think about rebounding versus shooting free throws in basketball. Think about putting versus a tee shot in golf. Think about skiing versus shooting in the biathlon. Think about passing the baton versus running in a relay race. Which of these skills would benefit from higher energy, and which from lower? The skills that benefit from lower energy are shooting free throws, putting, shooting, and passing the baton; those that benefit from higher energy are rebounding, hitting a tee shot, skiing, and running. Clearly, there is much to learn about identifying the ideal level of energy for you in your sport and relative to the skills that you have to perform.

In summary, your energy levels differ from day to day and exist along a range from low to high. Energy levels have an impact on your ability to attend to important cues that are necessary for you to perform well. They also affect your ability to execute the necessary physical skills for your sport. The key is to determine which level of energy is right for you so that you can perform at your best. Your next task is to learn skills that will help you get yourself to this level of energy before your competition.

## Identify Your Optimal Level of Energy

To identify the optimal level of energy for you, think back to some recent good performances and identify your energy level during those events. Reflect back on the last several months and identify a few competitions where you felt like you were performing really well. Don't focus on the outcome of the event; merely think back to competitions where you *performed* at your best. Did you feel that your attentional width was appropriate and that you were able to perform the necessary physical skills? Were you powerful when you needed to be powerful? Were you accurate when you needed to be accurate? Were you focused on relevant cues and able to ignore cues that were not important for performance? If you answer yes to these questions, then you have identified the competitions where your energy was optimal. Now think back to how you felt during those competitions. Were you relatively calm? Or were you relatively pumped up? Were you operating at a low or a high level of energy? The close relationship between energy and performance means that if you can identify the energy level that has been typically paired with your best performances, then you have identified the energy level that you should work to attain.

Some sport psychologists refer to this energy level as your "zone of optimal functioning," or just your "zone." The use of the word "zone" is perfect because it describes a state of performance where you feel like you are at one with the competition. Many athletes describe being in the zone as being able to perform without effort. They will say that they were focused completely on the competition and were not distracted at all by cues that weren't important for performance. Clearly, these athletes were performing at their ideal energy level. If you can identify your ideal energy zone, then the next steps will be to learn to identify your current level of energy and to use energy management skills and pre-performance routines that will help you re-create this zone for competition.

## Where Are You Relative to the Zone?

After you identify the level of energy that is needed to perform at your best, the next step is to become aware of your current level of energy before your competitions. In other words, you've just identified the zone that you need to be in to perform well. Now you need to know where you are on the energy continuum relative to the zone so that you can determine the appropriate pre-game techniques to use. For example, you may have used energizing techniques prior to every competition in your regular season, and they may have worked beautifully to raise your energy to the optimal level. These energizing techniques were necessary because your energy level was naturally low prior to these regular season events. But now you are in the playoffs, and your energy level is higher than normal and higher than your optimal level because of the excitement. If this is the case, for the first time all season, you may need to use relaxation techniques to decrease your energy to the optimal level. To effectively use energy management techniques, you need to know your current energy level so that you select the right techniques to increase or decrease your energy so that you reach your zone.

As you approach the competition, give some thought to your current level of energy. Is your heart racing? Do you feel like you have butterflies in your stomach? Do you feel antsy and excited? If you answer yes to these questions, then you are at a high level of energy. If you answer no to these questions, then perhaps you are at a low level of energy. Do you feel calm and relaxed? Is your heart beating at a slow rate? Are you thinking of other things besides the upcoming competition? If you answer yes to these questions, then you are at a low level of energy.

## Managing Your Energy Levels — Getting into the Zone

So now that you have identified the zone that you need to strive for and you know how to assess your current level of energy, the next step is to learn to manage your energy so that you can put yourself into your zone consistently before competitions. Think back again to those instances where you felt your energy was perfect and you performed very well.

Do you remember what you did prior to that competition or what happened during competition that resulted in your energy being what it was? If you do, this may give you an indication of how to create that energy level again. Of course, this will not always be practical. If, for example, you had a big fight with a family member before your competition and that fight increased your energy, this is not a situation that you will want to re-create before your next competition. Instead you will need to find other methods that are within your control and easy to re-create so that you can raise your energy for competition when you need to.

## Energizing Techniques

If your current level of energy is lower than your zone for optimal performance, then you will want to use energizing techniques. Energizing techniques include being physically active, cheering, using imagery to pump yourself up, and listening to music. For example, some athletes will perform high-intensity physical warm-ups prior to competition; this loosens and warms the muscles and increases energy by elevating heart rate. For example, you may warm up slowly initially and do some stretching with your teammates, but immediately before the competition, you may run several sprints to energize yourself so that you get into your zone.

Other athletes use cheering and chanting to fire themselves up prior to an event. They cheer loudly for their teammates, perform chants prior to the competition to get psyched up, or use phrases like "Come on!!" to fire up themselves and others. Other athletes may use imagery (see Chapter 14) to get themselves energized for their performance. While traveling to a competition or stretching before an event, they visualize their performance and imagine themselves full of energy and ready to go. The key with this kind of imagery is that the feelings of the appropriate energy level have to be incorporated into your visual images of yourself performing well. That is, when you use imagery to energize yourself, you visualize yourself being excited and enthusiastic and ready to go. Other athletes will listen to music to pump themselves up. Michael Phelps, a swimmer who won eight gold medals in the 2008 Olympics, used rap music to pump himself up prior to a race. According to Michael, "I always have on my headphones to block out all of the other distractions and I'm just focused on doing the best that I can. . . . There are a few of them . . . DMX 'Party Up' . . . Mack 10, BC, and Ice Cube 'Connected for Life.' I also listen to the Eminem CD . . . whichever song really gets me going that night."

### Calming Techniques

Calming techniques should be used when your current level of energy is higher than the zone that you've identified as being optimal. Calming techniques include breathing exercises, imagery, listening to music, and stretching. You may often see athletes performing breathing exercises prior to the performance of a particular event in their sport. For example, you frequently see basketball players take a deep breath prior to shooting a free throw, and you certainly see marksmen focus on controlling their breathing as they shoot at the target. At its simplest, the idea is to breathe slowly and deeply and to free your mind of worry. Some athletes may also combine their breathing exercises with imagery (see Chapter 14). With gymnasts, you can almost see this happening. They take several deep breaths and may even close their eyes as they visualize themselves performing the event perfectly. In fact, sometimes you will see them moving slightly or leaning in the direction that they are imagining in their mind. Imagery can be used as just described in combination with breathing, or it can be used by itself. To use imagery as a calming technique, you may imagine a tranquil scene, such as sitting beside a peaceful lake on a cool day. Or you may imagine yourself being completely relaxed and calmly stepping toward your performance.

Listening to music can also be used as a calming tool. You simply select music that you find peaceful and relaxing and then listen to that music before your competition. You may combine the music with breathing, imagery, or both. Finally, stretching may also be a time when athletes can calm their energy. All of these methods are designed to slow heart and breathing rates so that you feel physically calmer, and they are also designed to distract you from the stressors surrounding the event itself (e.g., the other team's players chanting or cheering).

### Emotional Techniques

Some athletes will also use their emotions to help get them into their zone. In my experiences working with athletes, this has typically not been the most consistently effective means of getting into the zone, largely because emotions are not very long-lasting and are not completely under the athlete's control.

For example, I once worked with a soccer player named Antonio who could not get himself to the optimal energy state for performance until he got into a physical confrontation in the game that resulted in him getting angry. Because he realized that this was the case, he would spend the first part of the game attempting to get into a physical confrontation with one of his opponents so that he could achieve the desired effect and get into his zone. Once Antonio got angry, his energy would increase and he would perform at his best. However, the use of anger to achieve the appropriate energy level was not working well—this method was not completely in Antonio's control, meant that Antonio wasn't ready to play when the game began, and contributed to Antonio's reputation as a dirty player. These limitations on Antonio's ability to get himself into his zone using anger motivated him to learn other energy management techniques that he could control more completely and that weren't based on negative emotions. This is just one example, but it emphasizes my belief that the use of emotions to regulate your energy level is not the best choice, and I encourage you to use the energy management techniques described earlier in this chapter.

Once you have identified techniques that you believe will work for you, think about how they will fit into your competition and with your coach's pre-performance routines. If your coach likes the team to warm up together and to cheer and get one another roused up, then your desire to sit quietly doing imagery just before competition might not fit with the coach's goals. You might want to speak with your coach about your own individual needs in terms of your mental preparation so that the coach will understand what you might require in terms of adjusting your energy prior to the event. Ultimately, though, you will have to figure out a way to manage your energy at times that do not conflict with the coach's plans or with the rules of your competition.

## Practice Getting into the Zone

Once you've identified the energy management technique that works best for you, try using it prior to your practices and competitions. Make sure that the technique is effective for you and that you are able to control your energy using this method. If the method you've selected initially isn't effective, don't be afraid to try another method or even to combine methods. Once you've tried the technique and are able to manage your energy levels, begin to incorporate this method into your pre-performance routine (see Chapter 13). As you begin to get yourself into your zone on a regular basis, you will be rewarded by seeing your performance become more consistent, and you might be surprised to see how the outcomes you desire from the competitions also start to follow.

In summary, to ensure that your performance is at its best on a regular basis, it is important that you consider your energy level. Different sports, different positions and events within sports, and different individuals all require their own unique level of energy for optimal performance. As a young athlete, you have the opportunity to figure out what that optimal level of energy is for you and for your sport. This is your zone for optimal performance. Think of past good performances to identify your zone, gain an awareness of your current level of energy, and then begin to incorporate energy management techniques into your pre-performance routine so that you increase the frequency of being in the zone and the consistency of your performance.

## KEY POINTS

• Understand that energy ranges from low to high and that energy is closely linked to performance because of its impact on both mental and physical abilities.

• Determine your optimal energy level by thinking of past good performances and figuring out what your energy was like on those days. This is your zone for optimal performance.

• Learn to identify where you are currently on the energy continuum and relative to your zone.

• Incorporate energy management techniques into your pre-performance routine so that you get into the zone before the competition begins.

• Increase the frequency of your good performances by ensuring that you are in the zone before competition.

# Identify Your Zone and Techniques to Get You There

Think back to one of your recent performances when you thought you performed exceptionally well. It doesn't matter whether you won or lost the competition; just identify a competition where you performed as well as you think you possibly could.

Describe the event: _____

_____

_____

Now, try to remember what your energy was like going into the competition. Describe what your energy was like (were you energized or were you calm)? _____

_____

You have identified your zone. Write a word or phrase to describe this energy level in the center of the box below.

_____| ZONE = |_____

Now, think about what you did prior to the competition that resulted in the energy level you had. Describe everything you can remember that contributed to you being at that particular energy level for that competition. Evaluate the contributors to your energy level and plan to use those that are under your control and compatible with your sport in your energy management techniques.

_____

_____

_____

_____

Now that you've identified your zone, you should attempt to get yourself to this same level of energy prior to future competitions. You will want to gain control over your own energy so that you can consistently get yourself into your zone before competitions. This knowledge of your zone will be important as you develop a pre-performance routine (see Chapter 13). Imagine that you are currently more calm than you need to be for optimal performance.

*Current energy level*   | ZONE =                                    |

Describe steps you would take to increase your energy level.

_____

_____

_____

_____

Imagine that you are currently more energized than you need to be for optimal performance.

_____ | ZONE =                        | *Current energy level*

Describe steps you would take to decrease your energy level.

_____

_____

_____

_____

# Pre-Performance Routines

A pre-performance routine is an important tool that can help you further develop consistency in your performance. A pre-performance routine consists of a series of actions that you do prior to the competition, or prior to particular events during a competition, to prepare yourself physically and mentally for that event. You should use a pre-performance routine that gets you warmed up physically, that helps you focus on the important aspects of your game, and that helps you get to the appropriate energy level or zone (see Chapter 12) for you to perform well.

## Key Components of a Pre-Performance Routine

### Warm Up Your Body

Physically warming up prior to performing at greater intensity is critical to ensure optimal performance and prevent injury. Muscles that have been warmed through light exercise function better and are much less likely to be injured. Most coaches recognize the value of a physical warm-up and so will begin their practices with lighter-intensity activities and will include time for stretching. These same coaches will also encourage their athletes to use a pre-competition warm-up that is designed to prepare the body physically for performance. However, if your coach has not addressed warming up or if you are performing when a coach isn't present, you should include appropriate physical activities prior to a practice or competition that ensure that you are physically warm and stretched and are ready to perform at maximal levels. These warm-up activities may begin with a light jog and stretching, include sport-specific movements, and build up to maximal-intensity activities such as sprinting. The important steps are starting at low intensity, warming up for at least fifteen minutes (longer might be necessary in colder weather or when you are particularly stiff from previous activity), incorporating stretching into the routine, and building to maximal intensity.

### Focus on the Important Aspects of Your Game

Focusing on the important aspects of your game is another part of your pre-performance routine that a coach is likely to help with. To identify these aspects, you must first have a good knowledge of the technical and tactical aspects of your performance that are important for you to be successful. These key aspects might vary from event to event or from competitor to competitor, but they will typically include a focus on certain technical and tactical components of your game, which is often referred to as your "strategy" for the competition. For example, prior to the start of the game, a basketball guard might focus on her ability to get the ball to her post players, on her ability to break the press, and on her defensive pressure. Or a runner getting ready for the 800 meters might focus on his splits, plan to decrease his time in each 100 meters, and warm up with specific pacework. Identifying these aspects of the competition to focus on might be driven by your coach's strategy for the competition, your own strengths, or technical aspects of your sport that benefit from increased concentration.

### Achieve the Appropriate Energy Level

Getting yourself to the appropriate energy level prior to competition is something that your coach is less likely to include in the pre-competition warm-up, for several reasons. First, your coach might not be as aware of the importance of including energy management in the pre-competition routine. Second, the appropriate energy level is specific to the individual, which means that the correct energy level for one athlete might not be the same as what a teammate needs. Therefore, each individual athlete has to take responsibility for identifying the appropriate level for himself or herself and for getting to this level prior to competition.

In Chapter 12, you worked through an exercise that was designed to help you determine the ideal energy zone for your performance and to identify techniques that you could use to raise or lower your energy. You should incorporate these energy management techniques into your pre-performance routine. Your goal should be to consistently get yourself to the correct energy level so that you increase the consistency of your good performances.

## Developing a Pre-Performance Routine

Okay, so we've talked about the goals of a pre-performance routine. Now let's talk about the specifics of such a routine and how to develop one that is right for you.

Athletes typically use a pre-performance routine during the 24 hours before a competition, with an emphasis on the hours and minutes immediately prior to the competition. The pre-performance routine should be developed with an eye toward creating a consistent sequence of events that you follow prior to your competition; but you must also maintain flexibility in your routine, and you do not want a routine that is too complex. In developing your routine, remember that there may come a time when you are not able to perform a complicated, long, or very specific routine, and so it is wiser to develop a routine that you know you can complete. In addition, if you participate in a team sport, the degree of control that you have over the time period immediately prior to the competition may be determined by the coach.

As an example of an inflexible pre-performance routine, let me describe Isaac's routine to you. Isaac watches movies the night before the competition and goes to bed around 11:00 P.M. During the next morning, he does not think much about the upcoming competition. But he believes it is good luck to shower exactly four hours before the competition and then to play video games for an hour following the shower. Isaac then asks his mom to make him a homemade smoothie, and he likes both of his parents to drive him to the competition so that they can talk about the upcoming event. Once he gets to the site of the competition, Isaac likes to sit for twenty minutes to mentally prepare. Isaac is very fixed on the specifics of this routine and gets frustrated when he isn't able to carry out all of the steps in this exact manner. The problem, then, is that Isaac is unable to mentally prepare to perform whenever his routine gets changed the slightest bit. Imagine what will happen when Isaac has to travel longer distances for his competitions. Imagine if Isaac has to spend the night away from home prior to a competition. What will he do when both of his parents are not able to take him to the game? What will Isaac do if the coach asks the team to warm up together for the twenty minutes immediately prior to the competition?

Obviously, Isaac's pre-game routine is not going to be good for the long term because it is too long, too fixed, and too reliant on being in his own home with the competition nearby.

So what would a good routine look like? A good pre-performance routine includes activities that are easily repeatable and flexible and that prepare you for the competition. Beyond that and the desire to meet the three goals described earlier for pre-performance routines (warm up, focus, and energy management), the design of the routine is up to you and is going to be very individualized. But in a general sense, on the day before a competition, you will not want to do anything that is too physically demanding. You may spend some time performing repetitions of the skills involved in your sport, but you would certainly not want to do this to excess. You would also want to be sure to eat properly (a high-carbohydrate meal is recommended for endurance sports) and to drink plenty of water (obviously the importance of this differs between sports and seasons). In addition, you want to be sure to get enough rest the night before the competition. Relaxation skills (see Chapters 12 and 14) may help you with getting to sleep before especially important events.

In the hours closer to competition, you will want to pay even closer attention to what you eat, and you should continue to drink fluids as necessary. The idea is to be sure that you are fully hydrated and that you have enough energy for the competition but do not feel too full. Identifying the appropriate time to eat prior to an event will be somewhat individualized, but most athletes will feel comfortable and have appropriate energy stores available if they eat two to four hours prior to an event. For athletes competing longer than sixty minutes, it is typically recommended that you eat a meal that includes carbohydrates and easily digestible protein (such as low-fat yogurt, bananas, pasta, and bagels). Some sport drinks include both carbohydrates (look for 6% to 8% carbohydrates) and protein; because fluids tend to be more readily digestible than solid foods, these drinks may work well for you. In the hours prior to competition, avoid fatty or fried foods such as chips and French fries and avoid spicy foods that you are not used to. Caffeine and simple sugars (like you would find in donuts, candy, and sodas) can negatively affect blood chemistry and are not recommended before competition.

At the site of the competition, your routine should be much more structured. The exact actions of your routine will be specific to you and

By using a pre-performance routine that includes stretching and listening to music to relax, you prepare yourself to perform both mentally and physically.

will be designed to get *you* ready to perform. Some athletes may follow a routine designed to increase energy; some may want to mentally practice different aspects of the performance; and others may prefer to listen to music as a distraction and as a way to relax before the event. The particular format of your pre-performance routine is not important; what *is* important is that the routine be designed to get you ready to perform optimally and to improve the consistency of your performance. As a young athlete, you have the ability now to develop a pre-performance routine that you can use regularly to ensure that you are mentally and physically prepared for competition. Remember that the routine should be flexible and under your control and should include a physical warm-up, a focus on the important aspects of your performance, and energy management. Top athletes use pre-performance routines to prepare themselves for competition. Learn from them, but also pay attention to what you need to be prepared for your own optimal performance and adjust your pre-performance routine so that it is as effective as possible.

## Mini-Routines

In addition to using a pre-performance routine prior to the start of competition, many athletes also use miniature pre-performance routines (mini-routines) before performing certain specific events in their sport. These may be especially useful in sports that have natural breaks in play prior to the execution of a particular skill, such as shooting free throws in basketball, taking free kicks in soccer, serving or receiving serve in tennis, putting in golf, batting in softball or baseball, executing a dive, getting into the blocks for a sprint, or approaching the apparatus in gymnastics. If such mini-routines would benefit you, then develop them with an eye toward keeping them short and simple and within the rules of the game. Serving in tennis provides a good example of what I mean by keeping the routine within the rules of the game. The U.S. Tennis Association allows approximately twenty seconds from the end of a point until the server is expected to serve the ball to start the next point. Although this rule is not strictly adhered to at all levels, it would not be logical for a tennis player to develop a mini-routine for serving that was thirty seconds long. However, if you watch Rafael Nadal (one of the top tennis players in the world), you'll notice that his mini-routine includes toweling off followed by bouncing the ball several times before he serves. When the point is crucial, he will often bounce the ball as many as fifteen to twenty times. Since this takes longer than the twenty seconds allowed, he is sometimes given a warning by the chair umpire. Clearly, this is a counterproductive mini-routine because the last thing you want on a crucial point is to have your concentration interrupted by receiving a warning. That being said, many tennis players effectively use the time between points to go through a mini-routine designed to prepare themselves for the point. Most servers will bounce the ball a few times as they decide on ball location for the serve and focus on a technical aspect of the service motion. For example, I might bounce the ball four times, decide to serve the ball to the receiver's backhand, and focus on striking the ball near the top of the toss.

As a young athlete, you have the opportunity to develop a pre-performance routine and mini-routines that will help you get into the proper mindset and create a consistent, controlled mental environment for performance. I encourage you to watch elite athletes performing your sport to see if you can identify the mini-routines they use prior to particular events in the competition. If you have the opportunity to see your sport played at a high level in person, try to go an hour or so before the competition is scheduled to start so that you can watch the pre-performance routines used by the athletes. You will likely notice that they work with their teammates to warm up and that they spend some time by themselves mentally and physically preparing for the competition. Start using a pre-performance routine prior to competition and begin incorporating your own mini-routines into your practices and performances. The most important benefit of these routines is that they will make your performance more automatic, and once you begin to use them regularly, you are likely to very quickly notice improvements and increased consistency of performance.

## Post-Competition Routines

Another type of routine that many athletes use is a post-competition routine. This can be very useful for managing the emotions that you experience following a competition. In fact, many coaches will help with this through their own behaviors during the post-competition period. The keys to the post-competition routine are managing your emotions and focusing on the positive aspects of the performance. Clearly, this is easier to do when you have a successful competition (meaning either that you won or that you were satisfied with your performance). It is much harder to do when you felt that the competition was not successful (meaning either that you lost or that you were disappointed with your performance). Some of the work that helps with post-competition emotion management actually happens during the pre-competition phase. That is, if you worked to have a process orientation, have done everything you could to properly prepare for the event, and gave good effort, then you will likely be able to cope well with a less than satisfactory performance. Most coaches will also help you to manage your post-competition emotions by controlling their own emotions, by holding a brief team meeting following the competition, and by reinforcing the positive aspects of the competition. Athletes who are able to effectively manage their post-competition emotions take time to gain control of their feelings. They might stay in the locker room a little longer after the event, focus on the positive aspects of the game, and imagine themselves responding in a positive way to all types of comments made by parents, peers, media, and fans. By managing your post-competition emotions, you are showing mental toughness and are not wasting energy on an outcome that is now in the past. You may want to analyze, critique, and even discuss a performance that was less than satisfactory, but this should be done after a little time has passed and everyone's emotions are back on an even keel.

## KEY POINTS

• The use of a pre-performance routine will help you prepare physically and mentally for performance. This in turn will lead to consistent performance.

• Develop a pre-performance routine that is easily repeatable, flexible, and general and that includes a physical warm-up, time to focus on the important aspects of your performance, and appropriate energy management for you.

• Develop miniature pre-performance routines (mini-routines) that you use before specific events in your sport. These routines should be short and simple. By using these routines, you increase the likelihood of good performance and you increase your consistency.

# Develop Your Own Pre-Performance Routine

### Steps to Follow in the Development of a Pre-Competition Routine

1. Identify the energy level that represents the correct zone for you to have a good performance.

2. Identify the aspects of the game that you need to focus on.

3. Develop a pre-performance routine that begins 24 hours prior to competition and that takes you through to the start of the competition (see below for an example of a pre-performance routine). Be sure to include

    a. a physical warm-up;

    b. a focus on important components of the game;

    c. techniques that will get you to the appropriate energy level.

4. Use the pre-game routine before competition. Judge whether or not it was effective for you. Modify if necessary.

### Example of a Good Pre-Performance Routine for an Endurance Sport

| | Competition Begins: 6:00 P.M. |
|---|---|
| 24 hours before | Eat high-carbohydrate meal, drink plenty of water, go to bed around 10:00 P.M., practice relaxation techniques, fall asleep before midnight |
| 10 hours before (8:00 A.M.) | Eat high-carbohydrate breakfast, drink plenty of water, light practice session |
| 6 hours before (12:00 P.M.) | Eat high-carbohydrate lunch, drink plenty of water, mental practice for 30 min. |
| 3 hours before (3:00 P.M.) | Light snack of only carbohydrates; continue drinking fluids; get ready to go, gear packed, last visiting with family/friends |
| 1 hour before (5:00 P.M.) | Follow the steps of your individualized pre-performance routine: 1. Light jog 2. Stretching 3. Movements needed for the sport at slow speed 4. Stretching and mental imagery 5. Movements needed for the sport at faster speed 6. Stretching and mental imagery |

7. Movements needed for the sport at full speed
8. Stretching and mental imagery
9. Final conversation with your coach about strategy
10. Mental imagery/energy management/final hydration

### Develop a Pre-Performance Routine That Will Work Well for You

*My Pre-Performance Routine*

Competition Begins: 6:00 P.M. _____

24 hours before          _____

_____

10 hours before (8:00 A.M.)   _____

_____

6 hours before (12:00 P.M.)   _____

_____

3 hours before (3:00 P.M.)    _____

_____

1 hour before (5:00 P.M.)    Follow the steps of your individualized pre-performance routine:

1.

2.

3.

4.

5.

6.

7.

8.

9.

10.

# 14

# Imagery

Imagery is a mental skill that will be very important to you as you strive to develop your mental toughness. Imagery, which is also called mental practice, describes the process of imagining yourself performing certain activities. In other words, you do not actually perform the activities, but rather, you see yourself performing them in your mind's eye. Imagery is a technique that elite athletes use on a regular basis. Athletes use imagery as an energy management technique to calm themselves and to help them sleep, to practice performing sport skills, to prepare for performance in unfamiliar settings, and to practice performing in situations that occur infrequently in their sports. There is great variability in how and when elite athletes use imagery. But we know that almost all elite athletes use imagery as a part of their preparations for competition. In fact, many elite athletes even report having vivid dreams of their performances, and this may represent a form of imagery that also aids performance. Let's learn more about imagery; we'll begin by exploring how to use it for relaxation.

## Imagery for Relaxation

Imagery can be used as a calming technique to manage your energy level prior to performance, and it can even be used to calm yourself enough to help you fall asleep (this might be especially helpful on a night before an important competition). Relaxation techniques were introduced in Chapter 12, and I pointed out then that many of these techniques combine breathing slowly with imagery. Let me provide some more detailed information about using imagery for relaxation. Some of the steps that you will follow for relaxation will also be employed when you use imagery for other purposes. In general, imagery is enhanced when you are in a comfortable position, slow your breathing, incorporate all of your senses, and make the imagery as vivid as possible.

To use imagery for calming purposes, you will be combining breathing techniques with peaceful imagery. If you are using these techniques to help you to fall asleep, then as a first step you should get yourself prepared for sleep and be in your bed ready to call it a night. If you are using these techniques to calm yourself before a competition, simply get into a comfortable position away from distractions as much as possible.

The next step is to focus on your breathing. First, you should try to slow your breathing and to take a moderate-sized inhale followed by a long, slow exhale. Don't work too hard to take huge breaths or you will actually increase your energy level. Instead, just gently slow your breathing and breathe deeply and fully. If you are having trouble finding the right speed of breathing, try thinking about how your breathing sounds and feels when you are very relaxed and about to fall asleep, and then allow your breathing to slow and deepen to that same pattern. If you have a watch that displays seconds, you can use this to help you as well. Breathe in and out so that one cycle takes approximately six seconds. Once you are breathing in this pattern, then you can choose from a variety of imagery techniques to calm yourself. Once you find a technique that works for you, stick with it so that you become skilled in using it to relax.

## Peaceful Scene

Imaging a peaceful scene is a mental practice technique that was briefly mentioned in Chapter 12. Many people choose to imagine beautiful natural places. For example, you could imagine lying on a comfortable blanket under a large shade tree in a cool, quiet meadow. Or, you could imagine lying on a lounge chair at the beach on a comfortable spring day listening to the sound of the water peacefully lapping against the shore. When you choose the scene, be sure you choose a comfortable and relaxing one and not one that provokes anxiety. For example, it would not make sense to image yourself lying on the beach on a blistering hot day with sharks swimming by!

Instead of imaging a natural place, you may want to image a special room that is *your* imaginary calming room. My calming room is a cool room with deep, dark green shag carpeting. It has a huge comfortable tan sofa right in the middle, and gentle music plays softly from a surround-sound system. When I use this room in my relaxation techniques, I see and feel myself lying on this comfy sofa.

Once you have identified the setting that seems best for you to use for your calming imagery, then you should use this image in conjunction with other steps to help you get into the relaxed state that you desire. The steps you use may depend on how relaxed you would like to be. For example, when I am using imagery for calming before a performance, I simply use the breathing techniques and the image of the calming room that I just described. However, when I am using imagery techniques to enter a deeper state of relaxation such as to help me fall asleep, then I do more. Sometimes "more" can be simply imagining how I feel when I want to take a nap—you know how that drowsy feeling comes over you? I try to re-create that feeling. I simply get comfortable, use the breathing techniques, image myself in my calming room, and then try to breathe and feel as if I am on the edge of drifting off into a nap.

Sometimes, however, I have to do a little more to get to a deep state of relaxation. In these cases, I use an elevator image to further help me to get to a deep state of relaxation. While breathing slowly, imagine that you are on an elevator that shows lights across the top representing the floors—7 6 5 4 3 2 1. When you begin, imagine that you are on the seventh floor and you see the number 7 lit up at the top of the elevator doors. As you imagine descending to the sixth floor, you say to yourself, "I am feeling calmer and calmer." As you imagine descending to the fifth floor (envision the light changing above the elevator door), you say to yourself, "I am very relaxed." At the fourth floor, allow the tension to leave your body and think, "I am free of worry." At the third floor, allow your arms, legs, and body to feel heavy and relaxed and say to yourself, "My body is feeling pleasantly heavy." At the second floor, you are breathing easily and deeply and feel very relaxed. At the first floor, the doors open and you lie down gently on your big sofa. You sink into the sofa, relaxed, quiet, and calm. Continue to breathe slowly. After a little practice, you will be surprised to find that you might fall asleep before you even reach the first floor of your imaginary elevator.

## Rose

Imagery of something other than a peaceful scene works more effectively for some people. An alternative technique that you might want to use for calming is to envision a beautiful pink rose. Breathe deeply and slowly and imagine one of the rose petals falling away. Feel yourself becoming more relaxed as you imagine another petal falling away. Continue to use the same phrases as in the previous example, but pair each phrase with a rose petal falling away until your imaginary rose has dropped all of its petals and you are completely and fully relaxed.

## Imagery to Practice Performing Sport Skills

In addition to using imagery as a calming technique, athletes also use it to help them practice performing the skills of their sport. The wonderful thing about using imagery is that when you imagine yourself performing, the body responds as if you were physically performing the behavior. That means that when you use imagery to see yourself performing a sport skill, you strengthen the movement patterns used when you physically perform the skill, resulting in improved performance. In fact, people who use imagery in combination with physical practice perform better than people who use only one or the other in isolation. When you use imagery to improve your sport performance, there are two important keys to making the imagery as beneficial as possible.

First, when using mental practice to improve performance, you should make the imagery as realistic as possible. You should try to imagine how the performance of the movement will *feel* while also imagining the *smells*, *sounds*, *sights*, and *energy level* that you will be experiencing. For example, if you are a baseball or softball player and you want to image yourself hitting the ball, you should incorporate the sounds of the spectators and the chants of the fielders. You should include the smells of popcorn, leather mitts, and freshly mowed grass. You should be aware of the positions of the fielders and you should clearly imagine the important details of the pitcher—for example, the windup, the position of the shoulders, and the release. You should see the ball clearly approaching you. You should imagine the energy level that you will be feeling. You should experience the movement and feel yourself striking the ball. Some athletes actually mimic the movements that they would be making during physical performance while they image the movement. For example, in imaging yourself hitting a ball, you could move your arms or shift your weight in the execution of the swing while you image yourself making contact.

When using imagery, make sure that you imagine yourself performing the technique properly. This step is critical because whatever you see yourself doing in your mind's eye will begin to become automatic, and obviously you want the automatic performance to be a good one! So to perform well, you need to imagine yourself performing technically well. Focus on the same keys to good performance that you focus on when you actually perform the sport skill. Use the same phrases in your mind that you use when physically performing. In our batting example, as you imagine the ball coming toward you, concentrate on having your back elbow up, striking through the ball, shifting your weight, and making clean contact with the ball. If you use self-talk when you actually perform, use that same self-talk in your imagery. For example, if you say to yourself, "Eye on the ball" as the pitcher is releasing the pitch, be sure to say, "Eye on the ball" at the same point in time in the imagery. By making your imagery as much like your actual performance as you can, you help to make the imagined movement automatic. Making the movement automatic is an important key to being able to perform the movement consistently well across a variety of situations.

Using imagery to improve sport performance is a mental skill that you definitely need to work into your training program. When you use imagery, you strengthen the motor movement patterns that are necessary to perform the actual movement (see sidebar 14.1 for an explanation as to why this is true). The result is that performance is improved. So when should you use imagery? You should use imagery for at least some part of every single day. Luckily, you can use imagery almost any time that you are not otherwise busy. You can use imagery before practice starts, during water breaks, before your classes begin, when you are going to sleep at night, or when you are riding in the car or on the bus. In fact, because imagery is not physically taxing, it provides a great way to increase the amount of time that you spend practicing for your sport. When you are training physically at a maximal level and want to add more training to your day, the solution is clear: add mental practice! The more you can use mental practice, the better. Combining mental practice with physical practice will result in *more* overall practice of the skills and will ultimately result in better performance.

In addition to using imagery to see yourself properly executing the skills of your sport, you can also use imagery to specifically prepare for situations that you might encounter in competition. For example, when the U.S. archery team was preparing to go to Korea for the Olympics,

Imagery can be used to practice your sport skills
even when you're just hanging out at home.

they used mental practice to prepare themselves for performing in this
new setting. They got a videotape of the arena in which they would
compete and used that to aid them in developing their own personal
images of themselves performing in that location. The mental practice
skills of the archers were so good that when they arrived at the arena for
the Olympics, many of the archers commented that they felt like they

# Why Does Imagining Your Performance Affect Your Actual Performance?

When talking about imagery, you might find it interesting to know something about mirror neurons. Mirror neurons have recently been discovered, and they might help to explain why imagery is so beneficial to performance. Scientists have discovered that when monkeys watch other monkeys performing certain behaviors, there are neurons (these are like electrical circuits) in their brains that are active. These neurons have been named mirror neurons because they fire in a pattern that *mirrors* the firing pattern of neurons in the brains of the monkey actually performing the task. The idea, then, is that these mirror neurons help the observing monkey to be able to mimic the task performed by the active monkey. These same neurons have been identified in infants who are observing adults perform various behaviors, such as brushing their teeth, walking, and opening a door. If you have ever been around toddlers, you probably know that they are constantly trying to copy the movements of the older children and adults around them. If you turn on the water faucet, they'll try to turn on the water faucet. If you use the microwave, they'll try to use the microwave. If you rock in a rocking chair, they'll try to rock in the rocking chair. What's amazing about this, though, is that the toddlers appear to have been studying the adults, because they are pretty good at trying these movements even for the first time. Of course, they haven't been "studying" adults, but rather, the mirror neurons have helped them to learn by watching. Because the mirror neurons fire when the toddler watches someone perform a behavior, the child's mind is preparing to perform the same behavior.

Mirror neurons have already been working in you. Have you ever been told (or noticed) that you walk or sometimes strike a certain pose like one of your parents? Although the genetic link is obvious, it is also likely that your mirror neurons have "taught" you how to walk or to strike the pose like the parent you have been observing your entire life. The links to sport performance are probably obvious to you. Whether you are observing a skilled athlete perform a sport skill or you are mentally imaging yourself performing that skill, the mirror neurons are firing and are preparing you to be able to physically perform the same skill better and more automatically. If you use imagery frequently, then the repeated firing of the mirror neurons will contribute to your ability to perform the task better when you perform it for real. The evidence is definitely clear that mentally practicing a skill can help you to perform that skill better and more automatically. And performing the skill more automatically will be very important as you are faced with a variety of situations and a wide range of challenges in your sport.

had been there before! One archer had such vivid and detailed imagery of his performance in the stadium that, upon arriving in Korea, he noticed that the flags at the top of the stadium had been changed. If you anticipate traveling to a competition, you can use imagery to help prepare for competing in that new setting. If you've been to that site before, you can combine your memory of the site with your imagery of your own performance to mentally prepare yourself to perform in that setting again. Using imagery to prepare for performance in a new setting serves the dual purpose of helping your execution of the sport skills and helping you to manage your energy level when you enter unfamiliar settings. Athletes who use imagery for this purpose frequently comment that the imagery allowed them to be fully mentally prepared for performing in the new arena, field, stadium, or pool. They say that the imagery made them feel like they'd performed there before so that they felt more comfortable and confident when the competition actually took place. This is exemplified by Michael Phelps's description of using imagery to prepare for the Olympic trials: "Before the trials I was doing a lot of relaxing exercises and visualization. And I think that that helped me to get a feel of what it was gonna be like when I got there. I knew that I had done everything that I could to get ready for that meet, both physically and mentally."

## Imagery to Practice Performing in Situations That Occur Infrequently

Similarly to using imagery to prepare for performance in new settings, elite athletes also use mental practice to envision themselves performing in situations that occur infrequently in their sports but that they want to be prepared to face. Some examples of infrequent situations that occur in different sports and for which imagery could be used include coming up to bat with bases loaded and one out, serving at match point, running the last event when the outcome will determine the winner of a track meet, being asked to take the game-ending shot in a lacrosse game, and having the puck in the offensive end with ten seconds to play. Because these particular events do not occur frequently in competition and because they are such specific scenarios, your coaches may not devote much time to practicing them. Even if a coach did make time to prepare you for these events, it is not likely that your preparation for a specific, infrequent event would immediately precede a competition in which you had to face that scenario. For example, a coach will not want to practice penalty kicks before every soccer game because this event occurs so infrequently that using practice time regularly to prepare for it does not make sense. But if you are the person who will be given the opportunity to take the penalty kick in a game, then it would be wise to use mental practice to prepare for this possibility on a regular basis. Elite athletes understand that imagery is crucial in preparing themselves to perform in infrequent, high-pressure situations. Begin now to incorporate mental practice into your daily routine so that you, too, can use imagery to bolster the physical training that you are already doing.

**KEY POINTS**

• Imagery or mental practice is the technique of imagining yourself performing in your sport—it is performing in your mind's eye.

• Imagery is used by all elite athletes, and many elite athletes even dream about their sport.

• Imagery is used for calming and relaxation, to practice performing sport skills, to prepare for performance in unfamiliar settings, and to practice performing in situations that occur infrequently.

• Imagery results in improved performance, in more consistent performance, and in more automatic performance and should be used in addition to physical practice.

• Use vivid and realistic imagery and always see yourself executing the technique properly, because you are going to perform as you imagine yourself performing.

# Imagery of a Sport Skill

Choose a skill from your sport that you would like to improve upon. Describe the skill here in as much detail as possible.

_____

_____

_____

_____

_____

Make yourself comfortable and use breathing techniques to get yourself into a calm, relaxed state. Imagine yourself performing the sport skill that you described. Incorporate as much detail as you can into your imagery. Once you have completed the imagery, fill out the checklist below with respect to the imagery. Visualize the skill several times and see if you can improve your imagery based on whatever might be lacking from the image on the earlier attempts.

|                        | Attempt #1 | Attempt #2 | Attempt #3 | Attempt #4 |
|------------------------|------------|------------|------------|------------|
| Can hear sounds        | _____    | _____    | _____    | _____    |
| Can see vivid image    | _____    | _____    | _____    | _____    |
| Can feel self moving   | _____    | _____    | _____    | _____    |
| Can smell scents       | _____    | _____    | _____    | _____    |
| Used self-talk         | _____    | _____    | _____    | _____    |
| Saw correct performance| _____    | _____    | _____    | _____    |

Once you have mastered the ability to visualize yourself performing this skill, begin to use this imagery on a regular basis. You will enjoy observing the improvements in your physical performance that result from the use of mental practice.

# Burnout

When you commit yourself fully to attaining a goal and that goal requires a great deal of time, hard work, and dedication, you may be at risk for burnout. Do you know what burnout is? Essentially, burnout is when you reach a state of exhaustion that causes you to lose interest in your sport and, often, to quit your sport altogether. Burnout is a physical and mental state experienced in situations where there is a heavy physical demand that does not let up, where there are high levels of stress for performance, and where the rewards do not feel sufficient relative to the costs. Burnout occurs in sport and is also common in certain professions such as coaching, nursing, and teaching. Burnout results from overtraining, stress, frustration, and a feeling that the rewards of participation are no longer there.

One of the most well known cases of an athlete burning out occurred in the 1990s. Jennifer Capriati was a tennis sensation who started playing tennis as a four-year-old. Even at that young age, it was reported, she practiced tennis as many as six hours a day. As a thirteen-year-old, Jennifer turned professional. As a fourteen-year-old, she was ranked among the top ten in the world. While still a teenager, Jennifer made it to the quarter-finals in three grand-slam events (these are the biggest, most competitive events in professional tennis because all of the top-ranked players participate). In 1990 she became the youngest person to reach the semifinals of a grand-slam tournament, and in 1992 she won the gold medal at the Olympics. But shortly after these incredible successes, her world came crashing down. When she was seventeen, the combination of the stress and pressure of professional tennis, the physical demands of her sport, the weight of the expectations that were on her, and the divorce of her parents became too much for Jennifer, and she dropped out of tennis. Jennifer's experience epitomizes burnout, and it happens all too often in athletics. In fact, Jennifer was described as "the poster child for burned-out sports prodigies" in a *Chicago Sun-Times* newspaper article.

Burnout, however, does not sneak up on you. Therefore, it is important for you to be aware of the experiences and feelings that come before true burnout is reached. If you can identify when you are having these experiences and feelings, then you can take corrective action. The period that comes before burnout is described as staleness, and it typically follows a period of overtraining. Overtraining is when you are working too hard physically and mentally in your sport and are not allowing yourself enough time to recover between training bouts or competitions. You can tell you are in this period of staleness if you are experiencing several of the following feelings:

- You no longer enjoy practicing or playing your sport.
- You are unable to reach your typical performance levels.
- You feel unusually fatigued (mentally and physically).
- You do not recover from training or games as quickly as usual.
- You constantly feel irritable or grouchy.
- You are not sleeping well.
- You no longer really care about your sport performance.

If you are experiencing the feelings listed here, then you may be in a state of staleness. If you experience staleness for too long, then burnout is sure to follow. If you feel that you are stale, then you need to make some changes so that you do not move from staleness to burnout.

There were likely some clear warning signs that Jennifer Capriati was in a state of staleness; but she might not have been aware of what these signs meant, or she might not have known what to do in response to these signs. As a motivated athlete with extremely high performance expectations, what do you think Jennifer would have done had she started to experience staleness? Since she was ranked in the top ten in the world with expectations of winning a grand-slam tennis tournament, when she was unable to reach her expected performance levels she might have worked harder in practice, believing that this would help her regain her previous high levels of performance. Can you see why this would be a negative cycle? Athletes become stale partially as a result of overtraining. When they can't reach their performance goals as a result of staleness, they are likely to train even harder because they believe this will help them to reach their goals. It is the physical and mental overtraining without sufficient recovery time that made the athlete stale, but most athletes (and coaches) will be tempted to respond to the signs of staleness by increasing the training load even more. If this is the response, then burnout is almost sure to follow, which is what happened with Jennifer. She was overtraining, she reached a state of staleness, and she didn't figure out how to lessen the workload, how to manage the pressure, or how to increase the rewards. So one of the top tennis players in the world dropped out of the sport completely.

Most athletes who experience burnout never return to their sport at a competitive level. Jennifer is extremely unusual because she was able to return to her sport and to reach a high level of play again. Jennifer took three years off from tennis and then experienced five years of up and down performances before she recovered her physical and mental strength and returned to her previous level of play. Then, as a twenty-five-year-old, Jennifer won three grand-slam tournaments and was ranked number one in the world. Jennifer was able to recover from burnout, but her case is extremely unusual. It is a testament to Jennifer's mental toughness that she did come back, and it was largely possible because she burned out at such a young age that she could take off for approximately eight years and still be in her physical prime when she returned. Nevertheless, just think of how successful Jennifer might have been had she *not* burned out and left the game. Think of the tournaments she might have won had she not missed eight years of playing at her potential.

So if you notice that you are becoming stale, how should you respond? The key to knowing what to do is to understand the factors that contribute to staleness. If you understand the factors that contribute, then you can make adjustments to address them so that you prevent yourself from burning out.

## Factors That Contribute to Burnout

### Physical Fatigue

One factor that clearly contributes to staleness and that ultimately results in burnout is physical fatigue. Learn to distinguish the difference between training hard with sufficient recovery periods and overtraining. This is a critical distinction. When you train hard with sufficient recovery periods, you will experience performance gains. This is what you (and your coach) are no doubt looking for in your training and practices. And there are times during the year when your training demands may be especially high so that you experience big gains in fitness. This is especially typical in sports like track and swimming where coaches purposefully include periods of high-volume, high-intensity training followed by a tapering period designed to allow the athlete to recover maximally prior to a competition. Clearly, the inclusion of these high-volume, high-intensity periods of training may be important for you to progress optimally. But when you train hard without sufficient recovery periods, staleness can creep in, and performance can actually decline. If you are experiencing the signs of staleness, then that may be a sign that the physical load is too much for you at that time. If you are physically worn out from training too hard, traveling too much, and competing too frequently, then you are at risk for staleness. Once you accept that you are training too hard and too much without sufficient recovery periods, the solution is obvious. Cut back on the demands! Now, I can hear the reaction from players, coaches, and parents who say, "David cannot cut back on his training; he's trying to make the state team!" To this I respond, "If David does not cut back on his training and continues to experience staleness, David will burn out and will *not* make the state team or any other team!" The relationship is clear. Too much training, too much travel, and too much competing contribute to burnout.

If you are stale, then burnout is looming, and you've got to figure out a way to cut back. Maybe that means taking a day off or maybe it means taking a week off. Breaks of this short length of time will *not* have a serious impact on your fitness or your skill, and they may actually help your performance because you will be more rested, motivated, and happy. When you take these short breaks, make sure that they are real breaks. Don't exercise or train, don't watch games or films of games, don't worry about upcoming competitions, and don't even talk about your sport. Do something else: go to the movies, play video games, socialize with your friends, hang out at the pool, or spend time with your family. A break like this will refresh your motivation and will allow your body and mind to recover from overtraining.

If you need a longer break from your sport, then I encourage you to take it; but recognize that it will be important to maintain your physical fitness during this longer break by participating in other activities. For example, Shelley is a collegiate field hockey player who is experiencing staleness as the end of the season approaches. In the off-season, Shelley spends the first two weeks taking a complete physical and mental break from field hockey. She doesn't play field hockey, she doesn't watch field hockey, she doesn't talk field hockey, and she doesn't train for field hockey. She allows herself to enjoy other activities and other forms of entertainment and revitalizes herself by socializing with friends and spending time with her family. During the next month, Shelley continues her break but recommits herself to maintaining her fitness levels. Shelley plays ultimate Frisbee, goes mountain biking with her friends, and lifts weights at the gym, but she continues to completely avoid field hockey. Then, after the long break, the preseason begins for her college team, and Shelley excitedly steps back into the game. She has given herself the chance to miss field hockey, and now she craves it. She returns motivated, energized, committed, and passionate about field hockey, and she has not lost anything in terms of her fitness or skills.

## Boredom

A second variable that contributes to burnout is boredom. Boredom can result when players have monotonous training sessions that do not incorporate variety or fun. At the University of North Carolina at Chapel Hill, Coach Anson Dorrance has a great solution to help prevent burnout in his soccer players. In the off-season, instead of asking his players to practice in the same fashion as during the regular season, he instead encourages them to play soccer in a different way every day. For example, on Monday the players are on teams of 2, and they play 2 against 2 in a racquetball court, using the walls to pass off of and playing a version of soccer tennis. On Tuesday, they are in teams of 4, and they play 4 against 4 on a basketball court. They use the court lines as boundaries, use an indoor soccer ball, and have goalkeepers defending large goals. On Wednesday, they play 6 against 6 in an indoor soccer facility. They play on astroturf with walls, goalkeepers, and large goals. On Thursday, they play 4 against 4 outside on the grass with small goals that are not defended by goalkeepers. By doing this, the team continues to play soccer during the off-season, but the game is different every day, and different technical and tactical skills are important in each setting. Since they incorporate this huge variety into how the game is played, the players are much less likely to get bored, and their chances of burning out are lessened.

If you feel you are suffering staleness and you see boredom as a cause, talk to your coach and figure out a way to add more variety to your training. Additionally, think about whether or not you are still having fun at practice and when competing. The top reason why people drop out of sport is because they no longer find playing the game to be any fun. Fun is a key to successful long-term participation in sport. Taking the pressure off your performance, putting the fun back into the game, and lightening up for a day or two in practice will help to prevent burnout.

## Stress

A third factor that contributes to burnout is stress and a feeling of a loss of control. Many athletes experience this when they feel pressure to perform well and when they are focused only on outcome (see Chapter 8). The pressures to perform well are just about inescapable in sport. They come from ourselves; from our parents, teammates, peers, and coaches; and at a higher level, from media, fans, and owners. All of these people and groups are likely to have expectations for you as an athlete, and those expectations can feel like the weight of the world. The key is to learn to handle these pressures and to appropriately manage these expectations. You will experience stress when you perceive that the demands that face you are bigger than the resources that you have to meet those challenges. Stress has a negative impact on you both mentally and physically. Your goal is to achieve a balance between the perceived demands and your perceived resources so that you experience a sense of challenge. To achieve this balance, you must learn to manage your perceptions of the demands and to manage your resources.

To manage your perceptions of the demands of a situation requires two skills you have learned in previous chapters. These two skills are focusing on process rather than outcome (Chapter 8) and focusing on those aspects of your sport that you can control (Chapter 11). When an athlete focuses too much on outcome and forgets to balance this with a focus on process, then the perceptions of the demands of the sport increase, stress goes up, and the risk of burnout rises. In the last tournament that Jennifer Capriati played in before dropping out in 1993, she lost in the opening round to an unranked player. Focusing on this loss and the failure to get the outcome she desired likely contributed to Jennifer's feelings of frustration, pressure, failure, and stress and was the proverbial straw that broke the camel's back. As mentioned earlier, you must be able to balance your motivation to be successful in your sport with an ability to focus on the steps in the process that will get you there. If you are feeling stale, refocus on process. By refocusing on process, you have the ability to experience success even when the outcome of the event is not a victory. This takes the pressure off the outcome of the event and lowers the demands of that situation.

The second skill is recognizing that you do not have control over everything in the competition. You only have control over your physical and mental preparation, your strategy for success, and your focus, effort, confidence, and concentration during the competition. And part of this preparation is recognizing when your performance cannot be as good as possible because you are overtrained. Had Jennifer Capriati understood that she was overtrained and stale and recognized that this was having a negative effect on her performance, she might have been more willing to accept the disappointing first-round loss. If you are feeling stale, recognize that you can only control your own preparations for competition and be sure to manage those preparations to address your experience of staleness.

The second part of the stress/challenge equation is that you must also manage your resources so that you feel they are sufficient to meet the demands placed on you. This requires that you be a responsible athlete and ties in with the chapter on balance (see Chapter 17). You should be sure that you are getting enough sleep, that you are eating properly, that you are using good time management skills to keep up with your responsibilities, and that you are training properly. Again, training properly means that you are training hard but that you are allowing yourself opportunities to recover physically and mentally from the training. You also should focus on keeping up your psychological resources. Make sure that you keep balance in your life by making time for your family and friends, by keeping up with your studies so that your academic performance is not a stressor for you, and by sharing your sport experiences with those around you so that they can help you cope with the demands you are facing. If you keep your resources high, then you will be able to handle the demands placed on you and you will be in a chal-

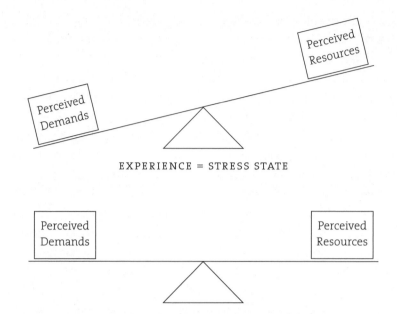

EXPERIENCE = STRESS STATE

EXPERIENCE = CHALLENGE STATE

FIGURE 15.1. The balance between perceived demands and perceived resources determines whether we experience a stress state (which can lead to burnout) or a challenge state (which leads to growth and improvement).

lenge state. This is a state where resources meet demands and where the result is growth and improvement.

By managing the level of stress that you experience in your sport, you will keep yourself in a challenge state rather than in a stress state. Being in a challenge state will help you improve as an athlete. Improving as an athlete will do much to prevent staleness and burnout.

## Burnout in Sport

It is my opinion that the number of athletes who burn out is going to increase in coming years. Why would I say that? Well, think back to the reasons for burnout: excessive physical training, lack of recovery time, boredom, stress, fatigue, and high expectations. Does this list strike a chord with you? My guess is that you and many other young athletes who are reading this book might be experiencing these things.

The reasons for increased burnout are somewhat related to our modern society and to the nature of sport in the United States. Let's talk about some of the reasons why the number of athletes burning out is likely to be on the rise. In a very general sense, I believe that burnout will increase because the demands being placed on young athletes are increasing.

Many athletes begin playing organized sports at an incredibly young age. At the tender young age of three years, children are starting dance classes, playing in soccer leagues, taking swimming lessons, playing t-ball, and going to gymnastics classes. Many developmental psychologists believe that this is too young an age to begin formally practicing or training for sport. At three years, developmental psychologists would argue, children should be "playing" and not training, not practicing, and not following the rules and directions put in place by adults. How long have you been playing your sport? At what age did you begin "training" for your sport?

Many athletes are playing sports that they did not choose for themselves. Often the activities are chosen by the parent rather than by the athlete. In other words, especially at a young age, children do not participate in activities that they selected; rather, their activities are selected by their parents. Do you remember if you chose to participate in your sport or if your parents made the choice for you? Are you currently playing your sport because you enjoy it, or are you doing it because your parents want you to do it? If you are motivated to play your sport, then burnout is much less likely than if you are playing the sport for someone else. As Peggy Fleming, winner of Olympic gold in figure skating, said, "The first thing is to love your sport. Never do it to please someone else. It has to be yours."

Also, at a young age, many athletes train for their sport year-round. Many athletes play their sport for a school team and for a club team. Many young athletes are on teams that spend time, money, and energy traveling great distances for competitions. How many months per year do you train for your sport? How many days per week do you train? Although as you get older you will need to spend increasingly more time training for your sport to reach the next higher level of play, you have to also remember that to avoid burnout, it is important to take breaks from your sport. This is hard to do in the current sport environment. As James Reston, American journalist and Pulitzer Prize–winner said, "There isn't a single professional sports season now that doesn't go on at least a month too long. Baseball starts in football weather, and football in baseball weather, and basketball overlaps them both." In fact,

When you start to believe that winning trophies is the reason you're playing sport, then you had better win them all or you are likely to lose interest in playing.

some coaches I've talked to argue that the idea of a sport *season* is a fallacy; the expectation today is that athletes train for their sport all year. I would argue that for many young athletes, this makes the sport season much too long and contributes to the likelihood of burnout.

Many athletes have high expectations and feel pressured to win at a young age. In most sports in America, there are tournaments and events on a regular basis even for very young athletes. When you are competing in a tournament and playing for a trophy, this emphasis affects everything about playing. In other words, if you are playing for the trophy, then clearly you're not playing for fun or for the love of the game or to improve your skills. And if you don't get the trophy, then why did you bother playing? Playing for trophies forces young athletes to focus on outcome when they should be focusing on process. And when you focus on outcome and don't get the one you want, it makes you question why you're playing at all (see Chapter 8).

I understand that it might be hard to balance what I'm saying here with your strong desire to get on the best teams, to seek out the best competition, and to practice hard and all the time. But, for you to be mentally tough and to stay committed to your sport and to have the best opportunity to be successful in your sport, you have to make sure that you do not overtrain and that you do not become stale and that you do not burn out. Once most athletes reach the stage of burnout, they leave their sport completely, and the likelihood of them returning is slim. Be aware of the signs of staleness. Be in tune with your own physical and mental states. Be willing to take a break when needed. Manage the demands placed on you and the resources you have available, and do whatever it takes to keep the fun in the game so that you do not burn out.

## KEY POINTS

• When athletes experience excessive physical training, do not have sufficient rest, are bored with training, and feel that they do not have control over their situation, they may experience staleness.

• If staleness goes unchecked, it can result in burnout, which is typically only alleviated by dropping out of the sport.

• Recognize the difference between training hard with appropriate recovery time and overtraining.

• Be aware of the signs of staleness (fatigue, irritability, lack of enjoyment, etc.) and take breaks from your sport when necessary to avoid progressing to burnout.

• To minimize the likelihood of staleness and burnout, you should keep the fun in your sport and keep yourself from becoming bored at practices, take breaks when you need them, and manage your resources (by eating right, getting enough sleep, and using tools of mental toughness) and your perceived demands (by focusing on process and on things that are within your control) so that you are in a challenge state.

# Prevent Yourself from Burning Out

Are your practices fun?

If so, what types of things do you do that make them fun?

If not, what can you do in your practices to make them more fun?

What types of things can you do in your practices to prevent boredom?

What stressors do you have? How can you manage your perceptions of these stressors?

What resources do you have available? How can you increase your resources?

Devise a plan to combat staleness in your sport. If you thought you were becoming stale, what would you do to adjust?

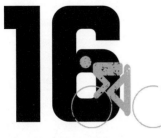

# Confidence Building and Maintenance

Confidence is vitally important for performance success in sport. Check out these quotes from elite athletes and high-level coaches that indicate how important confidence is to success:

- Terry Bradshaw (first NFL quarterback to win four Super Bowl titles): "What's the worst thing that can happen to a quarterback? He loses his confidence."
- Joe Paterno (head football coach at Pennsylvania State University): "You need to play with supreme confidence, or else you'll lose again, and then losing becomes a habit."
- Ron Tugnutt (former professional hockey player): "I don't think I'm any different from any other athlete. If you have confidence, you will play well."
- Jerome Bettis (former NFL football player): "You see an athlete look like a totally different football player because they've got confidence, they're playing with authority and they understand where they need to be. So it's not so much that they get better in terms of talent, but you can see the talent."
- Buffy Baker (former head women's tennis coach at Pennsylvania State University): "Confidence is a choice, and that's a matter of being able to block the distractions. Everybody has a poor performance. The better athletes know where to place that, learn from it and move on."
- John Calipari (head coach, University of Kentucky men's basketball): "The only thing I pay attention to with free throws is what

a guy does in the final four minutes of a game. If you can improve players' self-esteem and confidence, get them to relax, teach visualization and routine, they will shoot as well, or better, with the pressure on."

• Stan Smith (Wimbledon and U.S. Open tennis champion): "Experience tells you what to do; confidence allows you to do it."

How confident are you that you can perform well in your sport? I hope that you are extremely confident that you can perform well in practices and you have no doubt that you will perform at your best in competition. However, if your confidence is not high and you have doubts about your ability to perform well, you are not alone. At some time in their careers most, if not all, athletes experience self-doubt and a lack of confidence. While this is not unusual, it is something that you have got to learn to control so that you can be successful. All athletes experience moments of self-doubt, but athletes who are mentally tough do not let these periods of self-doubt last for very long.

Having a high level of confidence is important for a couple of reasons. First, confidence breeds positive self-talk, and positive self-talk helps to create a positive reality in your sport (see Chapter 10). If you walk out to your competition feeling confident, you will be saying to yourself, "I can do this. I am playing at my best. I will perform well today." These kinds of positive statements work wonders for your performance. By simply making positive self-statements, you create a reality for yourself that is positive in nature. Second, when you feel confident, this is evident to others, and this also has an impact on your performance. When you walk out to compete and feel confident, your teammates, your competitors, your coaches, and even the spectators can see the confidence in you and know that you have expectations for success.

Let me give you an example of how confidence contributes to your ability to be successful in sport through the impression it creates for others and through your own expectations for success. James has the opportunity to play in front of coaches who will be making selections for an all-star team. James is a good player, and he knows that the other kids who will be at the tryout are also good players. James has been playing very well in his recent practices and competitions and focuses on this fact as he heads to the tryout. James says to himself, "I am a good player," "I am prepared and will give my best effort," and "I know I am

By approaching a competition with confidence, you have an effect on teammates, opponents, and coaches.

going to play well." James walks out to the tryout looking like the most confident kid in the world. The coaches immediately notice James's look of confidence and put him on the field with the kids they expect to be the better players. The other kids on the field see James's look of confidence and think, "Man, I'll bet this guy can play," and they give James the ball on several occasions. Because the other kids are giving James the ball, his confidence remains high and he makes good decisions with the ball. James knows he can be successful and focuses on the techniques he has learned. The coaches see James's performance and they see the way he handles himself around the other skilled players, and these things factor into their decisions about who will make the all-star team. Can you see how James's initial high level of confidence helped to create a situation where his confidence was further strengthened and where he could be successful? This is a positive cycle that starts with a high level of confidence.

So how do you ensure that you approach competitions, tryouts, and practices with a high level of confidence? There are several factors that contribute to building and maintaining confidence. One of the most important things is to ensure that you have success in your practices. Being successful will increase your confidence, and increasing your confidence will help you to continue to be successful. Ensuring success is going to be largely up to your coach, but you should also be aware of the importance of performance success. Have you ever heard a coach say, "Let's end on a good one"? The idea is that you end a practice with a successful performance because that will stick with you and keep your confidence high until your next practice. This idea of ensuring success is especially vital when you are learning new skills, because when you are learning a new skill, you are clearly not a skilled performer. As an example, when young children are trying to hit a ball with a bat, they often first learn to hit the ball off a tee. This ensures that they have some success in their initial efforts. Once they learn to hit the ball off the tee, then the coach might begin pitching a larger ball to them. The coach tries to give a perfect and easy pitch every time to ensure success. Once the child has achieved a certain level of mastery, he or she will be asked to try hitting a ball that is pitched by another child who might not be able to pitch very accurately and who will be trying to pitch the ball so the batter cannot hit it. So if you are practicing on your own or even with a coach or team, be aware of the importance of setting up situations that allow you to be successful, and be sure to "end on a good note."

In addition to ensuring success, another key to building and maintaining confidence is to keep a record of your successful performances. Something that might help you is to keep a logbook of these successes. This logbook can incorporate your goal-setting chart, your pre-performance routine, and anything else you want. But above all, the logbook should definitely include your successes in your sport. And remember to judge your successes not just by outcome but also by process. So you may make an entry when you perform well in a practice or competition.

Remembering a past success is a great way to bolster your confidence.

You may also make an entry when you lost a competition but feel that you gave 100%. You can paste newspaper clippings into your logbook. You can also write in comments made by others. For example, if your coach commends you for working hard in a game, you should write this in the logbook. You should then review this logbook any time that you feel a lack of confidence. Look back at your accomplishments. Give yourself an imaginary "pat on the back" for your successes. Another popular way to keep a record of success is to create a highlight film of your own performances. If you have recordings of your performance in competitions and you are able to edit these recordings, it can be very helpful to create a series of clips of some of your successes in sport and to watch this video on a regular basis to maintain your confidence in your ability to perform well.

Another key to maintaining confidence is understanding how to interpret your own feelings of energy prior to competition. Think about how you feel before important competitions or events. Does your heart race? Do you have sweaty palms? Do you feel like you have "butterflies" in your stomach? All of these feelings are very natural prior to a big event. But the key is how you interpret these feelings and the self-talk that you use to describe these feelings. If your self-talk is like this: "Boy, my heart is racing, I must be nervous. I have butterflies and am worried about the game starting," then you are likely to start the competition with low confidence and poor performance. But if your self-talk is like this: "Boy, my heart is racing, I must be ready to play. I can tell that my energy level is just right. I have butterflies so I must be motivated to be successful and I can't wait to get this game started," then you are likely to start the competition with high confidence and with good performance. Clearly, you should learn to both control your energy level prior to competition (see Chapter 12) and interpret your energy level positively to maintain high confidence.

Lastly, comments made by people around you can have a big impact on confidence. If you have friends, teammates, coaches, and family members who are encouraging and supportive, then they are also likely to be making statements that help strengthen your confidence. For example, a supportive friend might say, "Great race, Lainey, you paced yourself very well." A helpful parent might say, "That was a really nice performance, Paige. You executed most of your routine perfectly, and I could see that you were concentrating on your technique on the more difficult moves. I think you have set the stage to be successful next week." These types of comments help you to maintain your confidence in your ability to be successful in the future.

If you take the steps described here, you will go a long way to building and maintaining high levels of confidence. However, it is important to remember that confidence requires constant attention and that even elite athletes experience an ebb and flow in confidence. When commentators are describing competitions, they frequently talk about shifts in momentum in sport. These shifts in momentum are almost completely related to shifts in confidence. When things are going your way, you feel confident, and when you feel confident, your performance improves, which further contributes to your confidence and builds a very positive cycle. When this happens, the commentators, fans, and your opponent will see that the momentum has shifted in your favor. What happens next will depend on what your opponent does. If your opponent has a high level of confidence and steps up the level of play, then the momentum may shift back again. And then it will depend on you! How do you respond when things are not going your way and it seems like your efforts are not being met with success? Do you remain confident and keep giving 100% effort so that things will begin to start going your way? That is what it takes to get through the challenging times in sport and to ensure consistent good performance.

### KEY POINTS

- Confidence is important for success in sport because it leads to positive self-talk (which creates positive expectations) and because it can be observed by others around you, who will then respond to you in a positive way.
  - Confidence is built and maintained in several ways, including
    - the experience of success—design your practices to ensure that you experience success, and be sure to end your practices on a positive note;
    - keeping a record of your successful performance—use a logbook and/or a series of video clips to record successful performances;
    - interpreting your energy levels in a positive way—use self-talk to positively interpret the energy levels you experience before a competition;
    - receiving supportive statements from the people around you—include these in your logbook, and use these to help keep your confidence high.

# Building Confidence

Describe a relatively recent performance success that you experienced. Think of either a competition or a practice where you were performing at your best. In your description, include descriptors of your feelings, your thoughts, your energy level, your performance, and comments made by others.

## *Example*

When I was playing in that game, it seemed like time slowed down. I felt so comfortable and graceful. It seemed like I could almost float around the court. I was energized and focused. I remember giving 100% effort and yet feeling like it was easy. At the end of the game, when I took the ball from their forward and looked up at the clock, I wasn't nervous or worried, I was calm and confident. I moved down the court and took the shot with 1.3 seconds left. I knew exactly what I was going to do with the ball the whole time. It felt incredible. Afterward, my teammates practically tackled me in excitement. Coach Perkins slapped me on the back and said he was proud of me. The players on the other team told me that I had played a great game. My parents said that I was reaping the rewards of all of my hard work. This success felt so good and gives me the confidence that I can play that well again.

Now describe your past success—remember, it doesn't have to be a game-ending shot, it can be as simple as a hard practice where you experienced improvements or a game where you gave it your all and performed as well as you could (whether you won or lost the game).

_____

_____

_____

_____

_____

_____

_____

_____

# Sacrifices, Balance, and Dealing with Disappointments and Adversity

All mentally tough athletes share certain key aspects. They have accepted the fact that they will have to make sacrifices to achieve their goals, they have balance in their lives that helps them to face challenges in sport, and they have learned how to deal with the disappointments and adversity that are inevitable in the pursuit of excellence. Let's talk about these aspects of mental toughness individually so that you can learn how to develop each of them.

## Sacrifices

If you have set high goals in your sport and if you are committed to reaching those goals, realize that you are going to have to make some sacrifices on your path. Now, you may wonder what you would have to sacrifice to be a varsity wrestler or a collegiate volleyball player or an Olympic kayaker, or maybe you've already advanced to a point in your sport experience where you understand what I'm talking about. Anyone who gives their all to the pursuit of goals in one area of their life will necessarily have to make some tough decisions (i.e., sacrifices), and those tough decisions might affect other activities that you might also like to pursue. As Frankie Fredericks (silver medalist sprinter in the 1992 and 1996 Olympics) described it, youngsters who want to be successful in athletics must be willing to make big sacrifices. They must give up activities their friends participate in, they must devote hours of time to training, they must expect to spend time away from their families, and they constantly have to be aware of what they eat and drink.

You may have to sacrifice socializing with your friends so that you can keep up with your studies and other priorities in your life.

### Free Time

The biggest sacrifice that all high-level athletes will certainly recognize is the sacrifice of free time. If you want to play at a high level, you will have to practice your sport for many hours a day and for most days of the week. These practice hours will involve both formal, structured practices and solo time that you spend working on your sport. Clearly, all of the time that you spend practicing is time that you could spend in other ways, so you are committing this free time to your sport performance.

Other ways that you will lose free time relate to the additional things that you must do if you are a serious athlete. One of these is ensuring that you get enough rest. Because you will need to be well rested, you will not be able to stay up late watching television or playing video games. To get enough rest, you will not have as much free time as some of your friends who are not involved in athletics. You will also need to have good grades so that you stay academically eligible to play on your high school team and have the opportunity to play collegiately. This means that you will have to make wise use of your time so that you dedicate enough study time to perform well academically. Between practices, studying time, and getting enough rest, you will not have nearly as much free time as your friends, and this may feel like a sacrifice.

## Social Opportunities

As a result of your commitment to your sport, you may also have to sacrifice social opportunities. For example, a big school dance may be taking place on the Friday night that you need to leave for an out-of-state tournament. To get to the tournament, you will have to miss the dance. As another example, your friends might be going out for pizza at 9:00 P.M. on a Friday night, but because you've got a game the next day, you'll have to miss this social opportunity to ensure that you get enough rest.

## Making Good Decisions

As a committed athlete, you will consistently have to make good decisions. In other words, you will be given the opportunity as a young person to make many decisions that could have a lasting impact on your ability to be successful in sport and in other aspects of your life. You may already be playing on a team that has clear policies that guide the behavior of the athletes on the team. When I taught at Wake Forest University, I always admired the Department of Athletics pledge of conduct included in the Student Athlete Handbook:

### PLEDGE OF ETHICAL CONDUCT AND SPORTSMANSHIP

As a member of the Wake Forest Athletics community, I PLEDGE THAT I WILL:

- ALWAYS conduct myself in a manner that represents Wake Forest University, the Atlantic Coast Conference and the NCAA with honor, dignity and respect.
- AT ALL TIMES demonstrate the qualities of civility and sportsmanship.
- KEEP MY PERSONAL CONDUCT above reproach.
- MAKE ATHLETICS A POSITIVE and valuable force in the educational and larger communities.

Some teams have policies that are even more explicit in that they might include statements describing how the coach might respond if a team policy is violated. For example, the state of Nevada has rules that make it very clear that any high school athlete who is involved with substance abuse will receive a six-week suspension from athletics for a first offense, a ninety-day suspension from athletics for a second offense, and disbarment from any further high school athletic participation for a third offense. When you play in high school, collegiately, or on a traveling team, you will have to stay out of trouble by saying no to activities that go against your team's policies. You will be in a position where your choices might affect your ability to continue to play on your team or to be eligible for a higher level of competition. As basketball coach John Wooden said, "Remember this, the choices you make in life, make you."

### Finances

You and your family may also have to make financial sacrifices because of the expenses associated with participation in your sport. The cost of sport participation can be quite variable. Track and soccer, for instance, do not require special equipment or facilities and are relatively inexpensive sports, but sports like golf, hockey, ice skating, gymnastics, and equestrian events are quite expensive. No matter which sport you have chosen, however, as you pursue higher levels of competition, the cost of training, coaching, equipment, team fees, and travel can become a real financial burden for your family. If your participation in sport is financially difficult for your family, you may have to make some sacrifices to help. For example, you might have to give up certain social activities like going to the movies, or you might have to sacrifice keeping up with the latest in fashion styles. You might even need to plan to earn extra money so that you can contribute to the costs of your sport. The challenge here is that when you and your family are strapped financially, the added stress can make it difficult for you to be in a position to pursue your goals. It is important for you to recognize that financial sacrifices are not yours alone and to be sensitive to the effect that your sport participation has on your entire family.

### Instant Gratification

Another sacrifice that you might have to make has to do with instant gratification. The efforts that you are putting into your sport are likely to have a long-term payoff but may not be as rewarding in the short term as you might like. Elite athletes have learned to put their faith into delayed gratification. In other words, the road to success in sport can be challenging and is filled with hard work, sacrifices, and commitment. Your coach might have a grueling practice schedule designed for you that is extremely fatiguing and challenging in the short term but is also expected to prepare you for the challenges of competition. You might be asked to incorporate new moves into your gymnastics routine that result in your not scoring well at local events. But you are then prepared to perform the new routine at regional events, and that is where you reap your rewards. Your coach might ask you to learn to play a new position, and you might not perform well there initially; but because you are willing to put your heart and soul into making the change, you develop into a strong player at that position and increase your likelihood of being able to play collegiately.

To pursue playing sport at a high level, you will have to make sacrifices. You will have to sacrifice your free time, miss out on social events, make good choices, possibly help with the financial burden on your family, and be satisfied with delayed gratification. What do you get in return for all of this? You get the opportunity to be successful in your sport when you know you've given it your all. You get the rewards of working hard toward a goal; the encouragement from your coach, teammates, friends, and family; the thrill of competition; and the joy of participating in sport. All of this will make the sacrifice worthwhile. All elite athletes have made sacrifices; the key is that elite athletes tend to view their sacrifices as opportunities and challenges. This is a mental shift, but an important one. The sacrifices you are making are well thought out, reasonable, and necessary for you to reach your goals. As such, they represent the opportunity that you have to be successful in your sport. As one athlete described it, "I wasn't bothered by having to miss my prom for training camp. I saw it as an opportunity to work on my game and have a chance to make the national team." As your mental toughness develops, you will learn to accept and commit to making the necessary sacrifices to achieve your goals.

## Balance

Although making sacrifices will be a part of your commitment to success in sport, you should also strive to maintain balance in your life. Balance sometimes gets lost as people work toward achieving challenging goals. It is difficult to maintain balance and to make the sacrifices necessary to be successful in your sport. The key is to be in tune with your own needs and to use the small amounts of free time that you do have to nurture the other things in your life that are important to you. Natalie Coughlin is an Olympic swimmer who provides a perfect example of this. Natalie won six medals at the 2008 Summer Olympics—the most medals won by a U.S. woman in one Olympic games—so, you might expect that Natalie is 100% devoted to swimming and that she spends all of her free time focused on her sport. But this isn't the case. Although Natalie is clearly a very committed swimmer, she is also a surfer and a cook, and she uses the free time that she has to keep up with these other interests. Natalie has said that these other activities help her to stay balanced, and she believes that participating in these other activities has made her a better swimmer.

As you increase your commitment to your sport, you might start to take time away from other activities that are important to you. As long as you continue to feel happy with your sport and with your level of commitment, and as long as you feel like you have an appropriate balance of your sport with your other interests, then everything will be fine. But there may come a time when you feel like you are becoming too focused on your sport and you begin to lose the sense of balance that you previously had. When this happens, you should pay attention to your feelings. If you need some time off to go to the movies or to attend a school activity so that you can reconnect with your school friends, then you should make this time. If you need to spend more quality time with your family, then you should make this happen. When you sense an imbalance, this should trigger you to recognize that you need to restore balance to your life. This is a challenge when sports are so demanding, but the maintenance of balance is very important to your success in sport. It is the balance in your life that will help you to get through the hard times and disappointments in your sport. If you feel that your life is not balanced, give consideration to the other aspects of your life that you would like to revitalize. Think about activities that you enjoy, and make it a priority to include these activities in your busy schedule. If you think you need time to spend with family or friends, make sure you find this time—be creative. If you feel like you need to spend more time with your parents, turn off the television and play a board game. If you need to spend more time with your friends, ask them to join you while you work out, or make a commitment to get your homework done efficiently so that you can take the time to go out for a pizza with them. Whatever it takes, be sure to keep balance in your life.

## Dealing with Disappointments and Adversity

Another important characteristic of a mentally tough athlete is the ability to deal with adversity. The road to success in sport is likely to include some stumbling blocks, and only by being mentally tough will you be able to move past these and use them to help you grow stronger. How do you respond when you lose in an important competition? What is your reaction if you are not chosen for a select team? Can you deal with an injury that occurs at a critical point in the season? If you are able to respond well to these types of situations, then this is a testament to your mental toughness—this will serve you well.

Let me give you an example of an athlete who dealt with a series of setbacks and who clearly demonstrated her mental toughness in how she responded to these disappointments. Karen Smyers won the World Championship for Triathletes in 1990 and 1995. Following these successes, Karen experienced a series of crazy accidents and medical issues that would have been daunting for anyone. In 1997, while Karen was installing a storm window at her home, the window shattered and severed her hamstring. In 1998, she was hit by an eighteen-wheeler while on her bicycle and had numerous injuries, including a bruised lung. That same year, she was diagnosed with thyroid cancer, which required surgery to remove the tumor and continuing treatments. In 1999, she broke her collarbone in a crash on her bike at an International Triathlon competition. The amazing thing about Karen is that she fought back from these challenges and won the USA Championship in 2001. Talk about a testament to mental toughness!

So how do elite athletes deal with adversity? The answer lies with many of the skills that you have already learned in this book: focusing on process, maintaining balance so that you can find strength from other positive aspects of your life, relying on your friends and family to support you through the hard times, viewing every setback as a challenge and as a necessary process for you to ultimately grow stronger, and recognizing that your goal-setting plan must be flexible so that you can make adjustments based on recent events. All of these skills will help you when you are faced with disappointment and adversity in sport (and in life).

Recent events in NCAA football provide evidence of athletes fighting back from a disappointing loss to refocus and achieve an important ultimate goal. In 2008, the University of Florida football team (the Gators) had set realistic and challenging goals of having an undefeated season and of winning a national championship. They started the season with three victories. Then they lost a game to the University of Mississippi (Ole Miss) 31-30. Following this extremely disappointing loss, team captain Tim Tebow described how he planned to respond: "To the fans and everybody of Gator Nation, I'm sorry. Extremely sorry. We wanted an undefeated season, that was my goal, something Florida has never done here. I promise you one thing, a lot of good will come out of this. You will never see any player in the entire country play as hard as I will play the rest of the season. You will never see another player push his team as hard as I will push everybody the rest of the season. You will never see a team play harder than we will the rest of the season." You notice that Tim's statement expresses a focus on process and effort, an ability to refocus on other goals for the season, and reliance on and inclusion of his teammates. Many believe that this loss ensured that the Gators would be focused and prepared for the rest of the season. They won each of the remaining eight regular season games by more than 28 points, beat the number-one-ranked University of Alabama 31-20 in the Southeastern Conference Championship, and went on to win the National Championship, defeating the University of Oklahoma 24-14. Clearly, this team understood how to use a disappointing loss to motivate them, renew their commitment, and regain their focus for the other goals for the season.

So if you experience disappointment in your sport or are faced with adversity as you strive to reach your goals, it is by relying on the mental toughness skills you've learned that you will be able to use these experiences to help you respond positively. As the Roman poet Horace said, "Adversity has the effect of eliciting talents which in prosperous circumstances would have lain dormant." Use adversity and disappointment to help you strengthen your conviction and your commitment as you adjust and refocus on your goals.

- To be successful in sport requires that you make sacrifices.
    - You will have to make sacrifices in terms of your free time.
    - You will have to make sacrifices in terms of social activities.
    - You will have to make the sacrifice of committing to making good decisions.
    - You may have to make financial sacrifices.
    - You will have to forgo instant gratification for the payoffs that can result by delaying gratification.
- Making sacrifices is necessary, but you must also maintain balance in your life.
    - Be in tune with yourself so that you can recognize when you need to give some of your time and attention to the other interests in your life.
    - When you recognize this, make time to pursue your other interests, to socialize with friends, or to spend quality time with your family.
    - This balance will give you the strength to get through the disappointments in sport and the resources to help you deal with the demands of sport.
- In the pursuit of your goals, you are likely to be faced with adversity and, at times, to have to deal with disappointment. High-level athletes use their mental toughness skills to get them through these difficult times, and the best athletes use these experiences to help them grow stronger.

# Sacrifices, Balance, and Dealing with Disappointments and Adversity

## Sacrifices

Think about the sacrifices that you are making to pursue your goals in sport. Make a list of these sacrifices. Now, examine each of these individually and think about how comfortable you are with this sacrifice. If you are comfortable with the sacrifice, then write down your thoughts about your comfort level with that particular sacrifice. If you are not comfortable with some of these, write down a solution for how you could minimize this sacrifice.

| SACRIFICES I AM MAKING | COMFORT LEVEL OR SOLUTION |
|---|---|
| *Examples* | |
| 1. Have not gone out with my friends on weeknights all season | Comfortable with this—I need this time to study and rest so that I am prepared during the week. |
| 2. Have not gone out with my friends on weeknights all season | Comfortable on Fridays—games on Saturdays. But, will start asking friends to go to the movies or out for pizza on Saturdays—this would help my balance. |
| 3. | |
| 4. | |
| 5. | |
| 6. | |
| 7. | |
| 8. | |
| 9. | |
| 10. | |

## Balance

Complete the following sentences by filling in phrases or words that describe yourself. Be sure to think about yourself broadly: Who are you? What phrases describe your character?

*Examples*

I am a soccer player.

I am a hard worker in practice.

I am committed to success in sport and academics.

I am _____.

I am _____.

I am _____.

I am _____.

I am _____.

I am _____.

I am _____.

I am _____.

I am _____.

Examine the phrases and words that you used to describe yourself. Do they all relate to your sport?

If you answered Yes → Think about what this means in terms of the balance that you have in your life. It suggests to me that you do not have great balance because everything you wrote down relates to your sport. Now, use the lines below to put in some other descriptors that do *not* relate to your sport. Give some thought to whether or not you might need to put some effort into these other areas of your life.

If you answered No → Good for you. This suggests that you have good balance in your life. Now, look back at what you wrote and think about the commitment you are making to your sport. If you have challenging goals in your sport, then some of the descriptors from the list should reflect a high level of commitment to success. If these are apparent, then you've got it all going on—balance and commitment—keys to success in sport. If the level of commitment isn't clear, use the lines below to add some other descriptors that reflect your commitment to success in your sport.

I am _____.

I am _____.

I am _____.

I am _____.

I am _____.

I am _____.

I am _____.

I am _____.

## Dealing with Disappointments and Adversity

Think about a disappointment that you have had to face in your sport. Or think of something that happened that challenged your ability to reach your goals. Describe this event. Then, list and briefly describe mental skills that you have learned in this book that you used (or could have used) to help deal with disappointment or adversity.

The event: _____

_____

| MENTAL SKILLS | DESCRIPTION OF HOW YOU USED THIS SKILL TO HELP |
|---|---|
| 1. _____ | _____ |
| _____ | _____ |
| 2. _____ | _____ |
| _____ | _____ |
| 3. _____ | _____ |
| _____ | _____ |
| 4. _____ | _____ |
| _____ | _____ |
| 5. _____ | _____ |
| _____ | _____ |
| 6. _____ | _____ |
| _____ | _____ |

# Dealing with Parents

Why a chapter about parents? Why in the world would a chapter about parents be included in a book that's written for young athletes? Parents aren't the ones who are playing. Parents aren't the ones who are upset about a loss or excited about a win. They are not the ones who are trying to reach their dreams. Oh, but now wait, those parents on that sideline do seem to be upset about losing and those parents over there seem to be incredibly excited about winning. And those parents act as if they are trying to reach some of their own dreams! That's why it's important to include a chapter about parents. Although you are the one pursuing goals related to your sport, perhaps sometimes it seems like your parents are the ones who are trying to have success in sport.

To write a chapter about parents is difficult. I know that there are some wonderful parents who are nothing but supportive of their children and their efforts, who care more about how their children play than about the outcome of the event, and whose children are proud to have their parents attend games and cheer for them. I also know that there are parents who sacrifice their time, money, and energy to make it possible for their children to be involved in sport. If your parents are like this, then you are very lucky, and I hope you appreciate all that they do for you. If this is you, then your involvement in sport is likely a positive thing for the whole family.

Unfortunately, there are also parents who have a negative impact on their children and on the entire sport environment. Some parents push their children too hard, emphasize outcome at the expense of process, and scream at their children, coaches, officials, and even athletes from the opposing team. These parents can have such a lasting negative impact on their children that their children are likely to lose their ability

Some parents are supportive and make your sport experience positive. Other parents are so negative and demanding that they take the fun out of it.

to enjoy playing their sport and may even quit. These parents can also make the sport experience much less enjoyable for coaches and athletes at practices and competitions. In fact, when I speak at coaching clinics, the most frequent questions that I get from the coaches are "How do I deal with the parents?" and "What do I do with parents who are making me crazy?" These are difficult questions to answer, not the least because knowing how to help coaches and athletes learn how to deal with parents depends a lot on the specific problem that the parents are creating. Let's take a look at some of the typical types of parents that might have a detrimental effect on the sport experience.

## Negative Parents

Parents can cause problems when they behave negatively. They may be negative only to their own child. Or they may be negative only to the opponents. Or they may focus their negative energy on officials and/or coaches. However, no matter where they direct their negative energy, the effect is that an unpleasant environment is created for everyone. So if your parents (or even a teammate's parents) are doing this, what should you do? How should you handle parents who are negative all the time?

One approach is to enlist the help of your coach. One way that a coach can assist is by creating the appropriate environment and rules for parents right off the bat. Many leagues and teams have an established code of conduct for parents that they ask parents to commit to at the beginning of the season. Others use a strategy whereby they ask the parents to help write a code of conduct for themselves—this is a great way to use peer pressure from other parents and to ensure that all of the parents are committed to conducting themselves according to the code they've developed for themselves. When I coach, I have a meeting for parents at the beginning of the season. At this meeting, I tell the parents that I and the team would love to have them come to the games to cheer for and support the team. I tell them that they may sit on the sideline across the field from the team and that they are welcome to yell their lungs out in support of the team or of a good play. But I also tell them that they are not permitted to say anything negative to any player, coach, fan, or official while at the games. If a parent begins to be negative, I will ask that parent to leave. If a parent is persistently negative, then I, as coach, ask that parent to quit attending games. So far, simply setting this tone at the beginning of the season has worked wonders, and parents have been only positive at practices and games. If your team has parents who are creating a negative environment, you should consider asking your coach to hold such a meeting or to help establish a parents' code of conduct, even if this has to occur in the middle of the season.

A similar, humorous example of another way to deal with parents was provided by Bobby Howe, the former director of coaching education for the U.S. Soccer Federation. Coach Howe was running a soccer practice at the U.S. Olympic Center (USOC) in Chula Vista for the under-sixteen regional pool players. As he was running the session, I noticed a group of people about one-half mile away on a big cliff that overlooked the fields. Coach Howe came up to me and asked, "Do you know who those people are?" I guessed, "Visitors to the USOC?" Coach Howe laughed and said, "No, those are the players' parents! I told them they could watch, but I also told them that they have to watch from that cliff! They badger these kids every day to practice and be successful, and these kids need a break to train in peace!"

Another approach is for you to address this head-on with your parents. I feel that I am on touchy ground here because I would never want to create a rift between you and your parents or to put anyone reading this book at risk by encouraging him or her to approach parents who may not respond in a reasonable fashion. So I will offer this suggestion, but I encourage you to use this method only if you feel like your parents will respond reasonably. It is helpful to address an issue like this using a technique that I call the oreo approach. The idea is to sandwich your issue with your parents (the cream-filled center) between two pleasant comments (the cookie wafers). For example, you could say, "Dad, I really appreciate you coming to support me at all of my games. I know you're my biggest fan!" (first cookie wafer). "But, it is hard for me to focus on playing well when you say negative things" (the cream center). "So, do you think you could keep coming to my games to support me, but focus on staying positive so that I can focus on playing well?" (second cookie wafer). The key here is to offer positive, supportive comments as your cookie wafers and to use the cream center to express your concern. Another key is that the second cookie wafer provides a solution to the problem that you are experiencing.

If neither of these approaches is possible or if you try one or both and they are not effective, then another solution is for you to view your parent's negativity as an uncontrollable factor that you must just ignore. Obviously this tactic can be challenging, but it is a reasonable tool to use to deal with your parents' negativity. You cannot control their behavior, but you can control your response to it. You can learn to tune them out when they are being negative and to focus instead on your game and on the things that you can directly control. When they say negative things, ignore the contents of what they say and interpret their comments as showing how much they care for you and how much they hope you will be successful. Use your own positive self-talk (see Chapter 10) to cope with their comments and to reinterpret what they say. For example, imagine that your mother screams from the sidelines, "Come on Janet, that was a terrible pass. No more mistakes!" In your own mind, reinterpret this statement to something like the following: "My Mom wants me to be successful and I did make a bad pass. I am going to concentrate on my passing and continue to work hard defensively."

## Parents Living through Their Children

Another type of parent who can cause problems is the parent who is trying to reach his or her dreams through your performance. Sometimes these dreams are for success in a particular sport, and other times these dreams are for wealth or fame. Todd Marinovich's dad provides an extreme example of a parent who wanted to mold his child to be a star athlete from the day he was born. When Todd was a little boy, his Dad started trying to teach him everything he needed to know about playing football. He talked strategies with Todd when he was three years old. He started having regular practice sessions when Todd was four. He shaped and molded him from the time he was a small child to be a professional football player. As a result of his single-minded focus on football, Todd was a very successful high school quarterback and was voted the offensive player of the year. He played college football for the University of Southern California and took his team to the Rose Bowl as a freshman. He was a first-round draft pick into the NFL and had a successful rookie season. Then Todd began to get into trouble for using illegal drugs. His drug problems became so serious that he was kicked out of professional football after his second season. Todd then played in the Canadian Football League and the Arena Football League, both of which are at a lower level of competition than the NFL. Eventually, Todd's drug problems were so severe and persistent that he wasn't able to continue to play professional football at any level. Clearly, Todd's Dad wanted the best for his son and wanted to give him everything he needed to be successful in football. But given his father's efforts to ensure his success, one has to wonder if Todd felt free to make his own decisions, if he really enjoyed playing football, if he knew how to focus on process rather than outcome, and if he had been taught the coping skills necessary to be successful in professional football. Perhaps Todd wasn't fully satisfied by his initial football success, and using drugs might have been a poor choice of how to cope with the pressures he was feeling. Perhaps Todd had everything going for him, but he finally got tired of working hard for a dream that was his father's more than it was his own.

So what about you? Do you feel like you are chasing your own dreams, or are you chasing the dreams of one of your parents? Make sure you know the answer to this question. If you are chasing your own dreams, then you're good to go. But, if you feel like you're chasing dreams that are actually your parents' and not your own, then you're going to have to figure out how to deal with that. In a general sense, when parents put pressure on their child to play a particular sport and to perform well, this almost always has a negative impact on the child. If you are experiencing pressure from your parents, then you are in a difficult situation. You may or may not still enjoy the sport, and yet your parents have made it clear that their goal for you is that you excel in that sport. What should you do?

Well, the path that many have taken is simply to quit performing well in the sport. Since the parents' goals are obviously outcome oriented, the experience of a long string of losses or poor performances may ultimately result in the parents' realization that their dream of success for their child will not happen. This is a solution that many young athletes have pursued either consciously or subconsciously, and the method has often been effective. The athlete begins to perform poorly on a consistent basis. The parents realize that their child is not going to be successful in this sport. The parents care less about their child's involvement in the sport. The problem is removed. The pressures are lifted. But this solution results in you not getting to play your sport. Playing poorly is obviously not going to be rewarded with more playing time from the coach. If that is not important to you and you are really only interested in how to quit playing the sport without having a confrontation with your parents, playing poorly may be a solution that is right for you. But if you personally want to be successful in the sport, this solution is not a good one. A better solution is to figure out a way to deal with or lessen the pressures applied by your parents.

One solution is to find a way to get some physical distance from your parents. At a high school level, many athletes will take the opportunity to go away to sport camps that give them a break from being under the

watchful eye of their parents, or they may discourage parents from attending "away" games. At the college level, many athletes will choose
a college that is far away from home, with the hope of gaining some
distance from their parents. There is nothing wrong with solutions like
this, which keep you on good terms with your family and provide you
with the break that you might need. Another way to get a break from
the pressure is to talk to your parents about overtraining and burnout
(see Chapter 15). Again, you may have to use the oreo technique to approach this subject, but if your parents' goals are really for you to be successful in your sport, then this explanation of burnout may help them to
see that feeling pressure to perform will *not* contribute to your success.

## Outcome-Oriented Parents

Another problem that I see with parents and with other members of
our society is that they tend to be very outcome oriented (see Chapter
8). How many times have you finished a competition and the first thing
your parent asks you is "Did you win?" The truth is that when you are a
young athlete, whether you won or lost is not even remotely important!
There may be some events that have important outcomes associated
with them (for example, a state tournament or a district meet), but I
maintain that when you are young, these competitions are really not
important. What is important is that you are having fun, playing hard,
improving, and competing at a high level. If you do these four things
in every event, then even if you lose every event, you will improve as a
player. And it is your continued improvement that will ultimately result
in you reaching the highest level of play that you can.

I recognize that this opinion may be completely counter to that of
our society. Children are being asked to compete in "important" events
from the time they are eight years old. And the reward that is given after
these "important" events is that you either win the trophy or you lose.
Winning trophies at an early age will not contribute to your ultimate
success in sport. In fact, the emphasis on trophies may merely change
your motivation from process to outcome, which will not foster success.
When you are very young or new to a sport, keep the emphasis on improvement, enjoyment, and mastery of the techniques and tactics that
are important in your sport. The way to be successful is to develop your
athletic abilities through practice and through balanced or challenging
competitions.

Let me tell you a story that illustrates how motivation can change from process to outcome and perhaps eventually result in a loss of interest and dropping out. A group of boys and girls have discovered an empty lot next to a beautiful old home. They decide that this is the perfect place for them to play a variety of sports. The first day, they play baseball and are having a great time, but the ball accidentally gets thrown through one of the windows in the beautiful home. The man who lives in the house comes to the door and screams at the children that they should not be playing there and that they had better not break another window in his house. So the next day, the group returns for a game of touch football. They're having a wonderful time when, would you believe it, the football gets kicked right into another window. Again the man comes out and yells at the kids to leave. Finally, the man gets a brilliant idea. When the kids come over the next day, the man says, "You know, don't worry about the windows. I've realized that I am enjoying the sounds of you kids having fun, so from now on, I'm going to give you each a dollar every day you come over to play." The kids are excited and happily accept the dollar each and head out to play. This is repeated for three days with the man giving each kid a dollar and with the kids enjoying playing in the empty lot. On the fourth day, the kids come to the door and the man says, "Well, you kids can still go play, but I'm not going to give you a dollar anymore." The kids are shocked. They look at one another and don't know what to do. They think about playing anyway, but decide that if they're not going to be given a dollar to play, then it's just not worth it. So they don't come back to the empty lot anymore because they now believe that the reason they're playing is for the money, and they have forgotten that they played for days just for fun. Do you see the trick? The man has cleverly changed the children's reason for playing from "fun" to "money." He got the outcome that he wanted by changing the children's reasons for playing, and it cost him much less than the new windows were costing him.

Unfortunately, this same scenario is being played out on sport teams across our country, but not on purpose. Most kids begin to play a sport because they enjoy the game. But then the leagues start to hand out trophies, and suddenly the focus shifts so the kids begin to think that they're playing for the trophies instead of for fun. What do you think happens if the trophies stop coming? Often the kids quit because they now believe that the trophies are the reason for playing. In contrast, people who continue to play sport for years get enjoyment simply from playing. They focus on having fun in their sport and on the joys of competing and giving it your all. You can't control whether or not someone gives you a dollar to play and you can't control winning trophies. You can control your effort, attitude, and focus during a game, and if these characteristics of a mentally tough athlete are in place, then you are likely to enjoy your sport and competition for years.

## KEY POINTS

- Parents can be hugely helpful in your efforts to be successful in sport. They provide encouragement, support, and even financial assistance as you strive to reach your goals. Be sure to thank them for all that they do for you!
- Some parents are not positive influences in the sport experience.
  - Parents who communicate negativity can hurt their children's confidence and enjoyment of sport.
  - Parents who force their own dreams onto their children often demand more of their child than the child wants to demand of himself or herself.
  - Parents who are outcome oriented can take the enjoyment out of the sport for their children.
- If your parents are not a positive influence, consider
  - talking to your coach about how to handle this situation;
  - using the oreo technique to discuss your concerns with your parents;
  - using self-talk to control how you interpret negative things that your parents say;
  - focusing on process rather than outcome so that you continue to enjoy your sport participation.

# Coping with Your Parents' Behavior

1. Identify the issue or concern that you have with your parents' behavior.

2. Explain why their behavior concerns you. How does it make you feel? How does it affect your confidence and motivation?

3. Identify someone you trust who can help you come up with a solution. This will often be your coach, but it might be a teacher, a sibling, or a friend.

4. Write out a way that you might talk with your parents about this using the oreo approach.

    a. Positive statement (cookie wafer)

    b. Issue raised (creamy center)

    c. Positive statement with suggested solution (cookie wafer)

5. Write out some self-talk phrases that you could use to help reinterpret your parents' behavior in a way that will help you to stay motivated, positive, and confident.

6. Write out the things about your sport that you enjoy and that are in your control.

7. Practice focusing on the things you identified in number 6 when you go to practice or competitions.

# Conclusion

In closing, to help ensure that your goals for yourself are realistic, I want to give you some information about the small numbers of athletes who actually make it to the highest levels in their sport. I was torn about whether or not to include this chapter, because I do not want you to think that I am ending this book on a pessimistic note. Quite the contrary, I am ending by reminding you of the importance of fostering your mental toughness so that you can give yourself every opportunity to reach your goals.

Because of the popularity of sport, the incredible amount of media coverage that is dedicated to sport, and the level of prestige that is enjoyed by high-level athletes, playing sport at a high level is a goal that is shared by many young athletes. If your goal is to play in high school or at a high level in your sport club, then I have every confidence that if you give it your all mentally and physically, you will put yourself in a position to attain this goal. Athletes who adopt the mental skills taught in this book and who commit themselves to their physical training will improve and develop as athletes, and the opportunities are there for high school and club sport participation. If your goal is to play in college, then this may also be in reach for you, again, with the proper dedication and commitment to excellence in sport and academics. There are more than 1,000 universities and colleges that participate in the NCAA, and they offer a huge variety of college sport programs. However, if your goal is to play professionally, then it is important for you to recognize that the professional opportunities are much more limited and to adjust your goals accordingly.

If you simply do the math, you will see that the chances of an athlete playing professional sport are very slim. Approximately 7 million athletes play high school athletics, and only approximately 400,000 play in college (1 out of 18). At this time, there are about 2,500 professional athletes in the United States, so only about 1 out of 2,800 high school athletes gets the opportunity to play professionally—these are not good odds! For women, the chances of playing professional sport are even slimmer because these 2,500 professional athletes are mostly men. Although the passage of Title IX has resulted in a huge increase in high school and college sport opportunities for women, professional leagues have, thus far, not stood the test of time. As an example, the first women's professional basketball league (the Women's Basketball League) was in existence for three years, and the next three leagues (Women's American Basketball Association, National Women's Basketball Association, and Liberty Basketball Association) lasted less than one year. The current Women's National Basketball Association has been in existence for twelve years, and I certainly hope that it will continue to prosper so that female basketball players have the opportunity to play professionally in the United States. Nonetheless, you should bear in mind that while playing high school and even collegiate sport may be realistic for large numbers of athletes, having an opportunity to play professionally will require that you are truly the "cream of the crop" in your sport.

I want to emphasize that I am not telling you these numbers to be pessimistic or to discourage your dreams. You probably realize that these numbers and odds were figured out mathematically, and they don't tell us anything about *which* high school athletes get the chance to play collegiately or *which* athletes get the chance to play professionally. I would certainly expect that it is only the mentally tough athletes who get these opportunities. By reading this book and practicing the skills described here, you are taking decisive steps toward developing mental toughness. Becoming mentally tough requires dedication and practice and will help you have the opportunity to reach your potential in sport. So if you have read this book and made a commitment to becoming mentally tough, you are putting yourself in the right position to give yourself that opportunity. Set your goals high, commit yourself 100%, and go for it. If you do that, then you have no reason to feel anything but proud about your efforts whatever the outcome.

Additionally, by learning the mental skills described herein and by becoming a more mentally tough person, you will increase your opportunities to find success in a variety of places. In other words, if you are mentally tough, you are likely to find success in sport, in academics, and in the workplace. You can translate the skills you've learned for sport into skills that will help you in other aspects of your life. If you are in high school, use your mental skills for sport and for your academics so that you increase your chances of going on for a college degree. If you get the opportunity to go to college, whether as an athlete or not, use your mental skills to ensure that you complete your college degree and position yourself for a satisfying career. I wish you all the best and congratulate you for taking these important steps toward the development of your mental toughness. Now, use your mental toughness to help you gain the margin of victory necessary to reach your dream.

### ADDITIONAL RESOURCES

For additional resources, please visit our webpages at ‹bringyouragamebook.com›.

# Acknowledgments

I want to recognize the U.S. Soccer Federation for giving me the opportunity to present sport psychology information to coaches attending the national coaching schools. It is through working with these coaches (and former players) that I came to realize that young athletes in all sports would benefit from a sport psychology book written specifically for them. I also want to thank Liz Etnier and Paige Wagner for their input and support throughout the process of writing this book. Lastly, I thank Sian Hunter for her encouragement and copyediting skills and Jeff Pill and Jonathan Metzler for their input.

# Note to Coaches

Although this book is specifically written for young athletes, the material presented here is also completely appropriate for coaches who work with young athletes. Most coaches have learned through experience that mental toughness is important for sport success. Many coaches naturally incorporate elements of mental toughness training into their practice sessions. Do you create gamelike scenarios in your practices? Do you try to get the most from your athletes? Do you challenge your athletes with the practices that you design? If you are doing some or all of these things, then you are already incorporating aspects of mental toughness into your athletes' training. But by reading this book and asking your athletes to read this book, you are taking an important step toward significantly enhancing the development of mental toughness in your athletes.

If you have not been formally exposed to mental skills training, then this book will be a great educational resource for you. Coaches who read this book will better understand the mental challenges that athletes face at different developmental stages in their training. Also, once you learn more about the development of mental skills and are introduced to exercises to strengthen these skills, you can begin to add these tools to your training plans and further enhance your athletes' development of mental toughness.

Once you've familiarized yourself with the mental skills that are introduced, you will recognize that *Bring Your "A" Game* is well designed for use in conjunction with your physical training programs. You might consider supplementing your training sessions and competitions with the mental skills training provided in this book. Imagine how powerful it would be to have your entire team working together to develop themselves not just physically but also mentally.

When you use this book with your training sessions, I would suggest having your athletes read one chapter per week. The chapters are organized in a conceptually logical fashion; to get the full benefit of the mental training skills for performance, your athletes should read all of the material included here. That being said, you may want to present certain material at key points in your season according to what you consider most appropriate. For example, many coaches may choose to have their athletes read the goal-setting chapter prior to the start of a competitive season. Goal setting can then be done by individuals and/or by the team during meetings with coaching staff to ensure that all are committed to realistic goals. Similarly, you might decide to ask your athletes to reread the chapter on energy management prior to an upcoming critical event.

After your athletes read each chapter, you might consider providing time to discuss the material as a team; I think this practice can be instrumental in increasing the rate at which the athletes begin to adopt the skills presented. In addition, depending on your setting, you might want to ask the athletes to complete the exercises provided at the end of each chapter. Although athletes will appreciate your offering to look at these worksheets to provide feedback, I would not require them to turn in all the exercises to you. That might limit their ability to be forthright and honest in their self-appraisals and observations, depending on the chapter topic. Developing mental toughness demands self-awareness and acknowledgment of strengths and weaknesses, and the chapter exercises promote the growth of these skills. However, these skills will only develop when athletes feel completely comfortable being honest in their appraisals, which very well might require a degree of privacy for some individuals on some topics.

By combining mental training with physical training, you will be amazed at how quickly your athletes can develop their mental toughness—as well as at the performance gains that are likely to follow. If you are a coach who seeks to improve your ability to foster the development of young athletes, I hope you will read this book and incorporate its lessons and exercises into your coaching. I wish you all the best as you begin to formally incorporate mental skills training with physical training.

### ADDITIONAL RESOURCES

For additional resources, please visit our webpages at ‹bringyouragamebook.com›.

# Note to Parents

*Bring Your "A" Game* is written to help young athletes develop their mental toughness through mental skills training. If you are reading this note, then it is likely that you are motivated to do all that you can to help your child be successful in sport.

You may wish to read this book with your child, or you may prefer to read it independently. Either way, understanding the key concepts described herein will help you better anticipate and comprehend the challenges that your child might face in sport. You may not agree 100% with everything presented here, based on your own opinions or experience, but I assure you that this material comes from cutting-edge research and is tailored to be developmentally and age appropriate. I believe that if you can accept some of the arguments that are presented in this book, then you will be better able to be a more supportive parent in your child's sport experience.

If you read the chapter on parents, be sure to identify whether you are providing positive or negative support for your child in sport. If you are providing positive support, then you are giving your child the tools, opportunities, balance, and encouragement to pursue his or her own goals in sport. If you recognize that your behavior is more in line with the negative parental behaviors, then this simple recognition is also a positive. If you are engaging in negative behaviors, I hope that reading the chapter on parents will help you to recognize the deleterious effects that your behaviors can have on your child. Self-awareness is a necessary first step toward change, so simply recognizing that you might be having a negative effect and accepting this point is important. If this is you, and you are motivated to change your behavior, please seek out other resources that are specifically designed to help you manage your emotions and behaviors in your child's sport environment.

### ADDITIONAL RESOURCES

For additional resources, please visit our webpages at ‹bringyouragamebook.com›.

# Index

10,000 hours, 29–31

Action-oriented goals, 58–59.
    *See also* Goal setting
Actors, 1
Adult athletes, 2
Adversity, 48, 63, 171–72. *See also*
    Disappointment
Agassi, Andre, 51
Age, 12, 15, 18–19, 23, 29–31, 36,
    41–42, 57, 145, 147, 153–54, 183
Agility training, 19. *See also*
    Fitness training; Flexibility
    training; Quickness training;
    Speed training; Strength
    training; Weight training
Agoos, Jeff, 61–62
Aikers, Michelle, 26–27
Anger, 4, 121. *See also* Emotions
Anthony, Carmello, 72
Anxiety, 4, 17, 136. *See also*
    Emotions
Archery, 115, 139
Arena Football League, 181
Attentional width, 110–12, 114, 117
Attributions, 6, 83–85, 87–88, 94
Automatic, 18, 19, 24, 28, 48, 97,
    98, 105, 131, 139, 141–42. *See also*
    Repetition
Awareness, 79, 97, 104–5, 122; lack
    of, 113

Baker, Buffy, 157
Balance, 19, 20, 41, 70–71, 76–77, 79,
    150–51, 165, 169–71
Ballerina, 18
Baseball, 11, 18, 23, 37, 46, 78, 102,
    104, 130, 138–39, 153, 184
Basketball, 9, 10, 11, 18, 20, 24, 29,
    30, 37, 42, 46, 71–72, 85–87, 110,
    111, 113, 116, 120, 126, 130, 153, 157,
    168, 188
Betts, Jerome, 157
Blueprint, 51–57, 59–60, 63
Bogues, Tyrone "Muggsy," 9–11
Bol, Manute, 9
Boredom, 28, 62, 149–50, 152
Bradshaw, Terry, 157
Brandeis University, 61
Breathing, 120, 135–37
Burnout, 19–20, 79, 145–50, 152,
    155, 183. *See also* Overtraining;
    Staleness

Caffeine, 128
Calipari, John, 157
Calming techniques, 120. *See also*
    Imagery: calming; Relaxation
Caminiti, Ken, 18
Canadian Football League, 181
Capriati, Jennifer, 145–47, 150–51
Carbohydrates, 128
Cassell, Matt, 40

Challenge, 2, 5, 6, 28, 38, 39, 48, 60, 71, 73, 78, 79, 116, 142, 150–51, 165, 168–71

Challenge state, 152

Chastain, Brandy, 98

Cheer, 58, 119–21, 177, 179

Cheerleading, 16

Chess players, 29

Club sports, 5, 36–37, 53, 74, 153, 187

Coach, 6, 24–25, 28–30, 36–43, 46, 55, 56, 60, 61, 78, 99, 102, 104, 121, 125–27, 143, 145, 148, 150, 160, 161, 168, 169, 179, 182; good, 5–6, 25, 28, 36–38; education of, 37, 178, 180; style of, 42–43

Commitment, 6, 31, 47, 57, 62, 75, 167, 169–72, 187–88

Competition, 1, 3, 4, 6, 16, 24, 26, 28, 37, 39–42, 48, 58, 60, 70–72, 76, 79, 84–85, 87–89, 98, 104–6, 114–15, 116–22, 125–32, 135, 139, 142, 143, 146, 148, 151, 153, 158, 160–62, 171, 178, 183, 185; levels of, 15, 38, 73–74, 78, 147, 168, 181

Competitive: challenge, 5–6, 40, 48, 155, 169, 183; team, 36, 53, 76; spirit, 76

Concentration, 6, 19, 24, 29, 30, 46, 84, 102, 106, 111, 126, 130, 139, 151, 162, 181

Conduct: pledge of (athletes), 167; code of (parents), 179

Confidence, 1, 52, 71–73, 83–86, 87–89, 94, 97, 98, 100, 104, 151, 157–63, 187

Consistent: effort, 5; performance, 48, 95, 106, 109, 122, 125, 131, 139,

163, 182; behavior, 83, 118, 126, 127, 167

Contract, 56

Control, 4, 6, 9–11, 13–15, 16, 18, 38, 60, 63, 84, 85, 88, 97, 98, 102–6, 116, 119, 120, 121, 127, 129, 131, 150–51, 158, 162, 180, 185

Controllable, 6, 11, 15, 18–21, 63, 88, 102–6

Coughlin, Natalie, 80, 170

Creativity, 21, 30–31, 170

Criticism, 29, 30, 47, 59

Cross country, 12, 16, 116. See also Track and field

Cycle: negative, 18, 95, 146; positive, 160, 163

Cycling, 12, 171

Dallas Cowboys, 115

Dance, 1, 4, 16, 153, 167

Debate, 1

Delayed gratification, 169

Deliberate practice, 30–31

Delle Donne, Elena, 20

Developmentally appropriate activities, 3, 153

Diet, 10, 13–14, 18, 51, 128. See also Eating properly

Disappointment, 60–62, 131, 151, 165, 170–72. See also Adversity

Disordered eating, 16–18

Diving, 130. See also Swimming

Dorrance, Anson, 149

Dream, 1, 5, 6, 11, 51–58, 60–63, 135, 177, 181–82, 188, 189

Dressage, 24. See also Equestrian; Horse racing

Drop out, 1, 71, 79, 146–47, 150, 184

Eating disorders, 16–18

Eating properly, 10, 46, 51, 151. *See also* Diet

Ebeling, Jan, 24

Effort, 3, 26, 28, 40, 41, 54, 57, 58–60, 75, 80, 85, 87, 88, 117, 131, 151, 158, 160, 163, 168, 172, 177, 185, 188

Emotions, 58, 97, 106, 120–21, 131–32. *See also* Anger; Anxiety; Stress

Energizing techniques, 118–19

Energy, 6, 28, 36, 52, 104–5, 109–22, 125–29, 132, 135–36, 138, 142, 162; management, 109, 114, 115, 118, 121–22, 126, 128, 129, 135

English Premier League, 30

Environment, 5, 25, 36, 110–11, 131, 153, 177, 179

Equestrian, 168. *See also* Dressage; Horse racing

Ericsson, K. Anders, 29–30

Ewing, Patrick, 9

Exercise, 10, 13, 14, 19, 125, 148; and sport science, 1

Exhaustion, 145

Expectation, 60, 83–85, 87–88, 145–46, 150, 152, 154, 158

Expert, 29–31

Failure, 39, 47, 57, 71, 73–74, 87, 88, 104, 151

Fatigue, 146, 147, 152

Feedback, 29, 30, 60

Fencing, 37

Field hockey, 12, 46, 76, 149

Figure skating, 11, 16, 153. *See also* Hockey; Ice skating

Financial sacrifices, 168–69. *See also* Sacrifices

Fitness training, 15, 18–21. *See also* Agility training; Flexibility training; Quickness training; Speed training; Strength training; Weight training

Fleming, Peggy, 153

Flexibility, 60–62, 127–29, 171

Flexibility training, 19–21. *See also* Agility training; Fitness training; Quickness training; Speed training; Strength training; Weight training

Focus, 3, 4, 9, 11, 15, 24, 28, 29, 30, 39, 47, 52, 57, 61, 70–71, 73–80, 85, 87–89, 97, 98, 100, 102–6, 110–11, 113, 116, 117, 120, 125–26, 128, 131, 136, 139, 150–51, 155, 158–59, 170–72, 179–81, 184–85; on process, 74, 76, 78–80, 150–51, 172, 181; on winning, 79. *See also* Outcome orientation; Process orientation

Football, 9, 11, 16, 19, 23, 29, 40, 115, 116, 153, 157, 172, 181–82, 184

Fredericks, Frankie, 165

Free time, 3, 6, 166–67, 169–70

Frustration, 1, 60, 62, 127, 145, 151. *See also* Emotions

Gable, Dan, 7

Garcia, Sergio, 76

Garibaldi, Rob, 18

Genetics, 5, 9, 13, 15, 19, 141

Goals, performance, 3, 4, 5, 17, 28, 30, 37, 39, 46, 51–63, 121, 145, 147, 165, 168–72, 177, 182–83, 187–88

Goal setting, 6, 51–63, 160, 171, 172

Golf, 52, 57, 74, 76, 84, 95, 115–16, 130, 168

Guenther, Heidi, 18

Gymnastics, 11, 12, 16, 18, 37, 60, 120, 130, 153, 168, 169

Hamm, Mia, 105

Hard work, 5–6, 12, 20, 25–28, 29–30, 39–40, 57, 60–62, 95, 98, 100, 102, 136, 145–47, 161, 169, 181–82

Harrison, Marvin, 115

Height, 9–15, 17; adult, 12–15

Henrich, Christy, 18

Hockey, 5, 11, 26, 30, 31, 143, 168. See also Figure skating; Ice skating

Horace, 172

Horse racing, 11. See also Dressage; Equestrian

Howe, Bobby, 180

Ice skating, 37, 168. See also Figure skating; Hockey

Illegal drugs, 16–18, 181–82. See also Steroids; Substance abuse

Imagery, 6, 62, 119, 120, 121, 135–39, 141, 142–43; calming, 135–38. See also Calming techniques; Mental practice; Relaxation; Visualization

Indianapolis Colts, 115

Injury, 4, 20, 47, 48, 61, 105, 125, 171

Instant gratification, 168–69

International Basketball Federation World Championship, 9

James, LeBron, 31

Jordan, Michael, 87–88

Kayaking, 165

Keller, Casey, 30

Khan, Jhangir, 25

Khorkina, Svetlana, 11–12

Knight, Bobby, 42–43

Krzyzewski, Mike, 42–43

Lacrosse, 12, 24, 143

Lewis, Carl, 104

Liberty Basketball Association, 188

Luck, 46, 72, 84–85, 127. See also Uncontrollable factor

Marinovich, Todd, 181

Marksmanship, 115, 120. See also Skiing biathlon

Maturity, physical, 12, 15, 18–19, 20. See also Puberty

May-Treanor, Misty, 12

Mean self-talk, 94–95, 97–99. See also Self-talk

Measurable goals, 58–59. See also Goal setting

Mental practice, 135–36, 138–40, 142–43. See also Imagery; Visualization

Mental skills, 1–4, 6–7, 48, 187–89

Mental toughness, 3–4, 6–7, 10–11, 46–48, 53, 57, 62, 70, 76, 77, 80, 84, 87, 88, 89, 95, 97, 99, 102, 104, 106, 132, 135, 147, 155, 158, 165, 169, 171–72, 185, 187–89

Mickelson, Phil, 76–77

Mid-term goals, 52–56. See also Goal setting

Mini-routines, 130–31.
   *See also* Pre-performance
   routine; Post-competition
   routine
Mirror neurons, 141–42
Missed opportunity (attribution),
   84. *See also* Attributions
Momentum, 162–63
Motivation, 19, 28, 38–42, 52, 59,
   62–63, 70–73, 146, 148–49, 151,
   153, 162, 172, 183–84
Mountain biking, 12, 149
Music, 29, 119, 120, 129, 136

Nadal, Rafael, 130
National Basketball Association
   (NBA), 9–11, 31, 46, 72
National championship (NCAA
   football), 172
National Collegiate Athletic
   Association (NCAA), 16, 29, 167,
   172, 187
National Football League (NFL),
   40, 157, 181
National Women's Basketball
   Association, 188
Negative attribution, 83–87.
   *See also* Attributions
Negative predictions, 95–99
Negative self-talk, 79, 94–95, 97,
   99, 100. *See also* Positive self-
   talk; Self-talk
New England Patriots, 40
Nicklaus, Jack, 57

Olympics, 11–12, 25, 28, 58, 80, 104,
   105, 115, 119, 139, 140, 142, 145, 153,
   165, 170, 180

Optimal performance, 115–16, 119,
   122, 125, 130
Oreo approach, 180, 183
Outcome, 39, 70, 83–85, 87–88,
   95, 102, 117, 122, 132, 143, 150–51,
   155, 160, 177, 181–84, 188; goals,
   70–80
Outcome orientation, 70–80,
   181–84
Overtraining, 20, 145–48, 151, 155,
   183. *See also* Burnout; Staleness
Owen, Michael, 51
Owens, Terrell, 115

Pan American Games, 24
Parents, 26, 36–37, 55, 58, 78–79, 111,
   114, 127, 132, 141, 146, 148, 150, 153,
   162, 170, 177–83
Paterno, Joe, 157
Pennsylvania State University,
   157
Perkins, Kieran, 63
Phelps, Michael, 25, 119–20, 142
Physical characteristics, 5–6, 9–21,
   23, 46
Pianist, 31
Poor Process (attribution), 87–89.
   *See also* Attributions
Positive attributions, 6, 83, 85,
   87–89. *See also* Attributions
Positive predictions, 95, 97
Positive reality, 97, 98, 158
Positive self-talk, 97–98, 100, 106,
   158, 181. *See also* Negative self-
   talk; Self-talk
Post-competition routine, 131–32.
   *See also* Mini-routines; Pre-
   performance routine

Pre-performance routine, 98, 102, 105, 106, 118, 121–22, 125–31, 160. *See also* Mini-routines; Post-competition routine

Pressure, 1, 3–4, 24, 39, 42, 48, 79, 115, 143, 145, 147, 150, 151, 154, 158, 179, 182, 183. *See also* Stress

Process, 74–80, 87, 150–51, 155, 160, 171, 172, 177, 181, 183–84; goals, 70–80

Process orientation, 70–80, 131

Puberty, 13, 15, 18–21. *See also* Maturity, physical

Pursuit of excellence, 165

Quickness, 15, 19–20

Quickness training, 19–21. *See also* Agility training; Fitness training; Flexibility training; Speed training; Strength training; Weight training

Rayfield, Janet, 78–79

Realistic goals, 52, 58–59, 87–88, 100, 138, 172, 187–88. *See also* Goal setting

Recovery, 147–48, 152; *See also* Rest; Sleep

Reese, Jeff, 18

Reinforcement, 55, 62. *See also* Rewards

Relaxation, 104, 118, 128, 135–38, 142. *See also* Calming techniques; Imagery: calming

Repetition, 24, 28, 40, 62, 128. *See also* Automatic

Rest, 10, 13, 48, 128, 148, 166–67. *See also* Recovery; Sleep

Reston, James, 153

Rewards, 40, 52, 54, 56–58, 62–63, 122, 145, 147, 169, 182–83

Ronaldo, 29

Rose Bowl, 181

Russell, Bill, 46

Sacrifices, 6, 25, 31, 36, 165–70, 177

Saylor, Billy, 18

Scurry, Brianna, 98

Self-fulfilling prophecy, 95–97

Self-talk, 94–100, 102–4, 139, 162. *See also* Negative self-talk; Positive self-talk

Short-term goals, 52–53, 55, 57, 60, 62–63. *See also* Goal setting

Skiing biathlon, 115–16. *See also* Marksmanship

Sleep, 13, 128, 135–37, 139, 146, 151. *See also* Recovery; Rest

SMART, 58–60. *See also* Goal setting

Smith, Dean, 71

Smith, Stan, 158

Smyers, Karen, 171

Soccer, 9, 12, 20–21, 23, 26, 29, 30, 37, 51, 53, 61, 78, 86, 98, 105, 121, 130, 143, 149, 153, 168, 180

Softball, 24, 37, 130, 138, 143

Southeastern Conference Championship (football), 172

Specific goals, 58–59. *See also* Goal setting

Speed, 9, 15, 24, 115–16

Speed training, 18–21. *See also* Fitness training; Flexibility training; Quickness training;

Strength training; Weight
training
Spelling bee, 1, 4
Sport Psychology, 1–3
Squash, 25
Staleness, 146–52, 155. *See also*
Burnout; Overtraining
Steroids, 16–17. *See also* Illegal
drugs; Substance abuse
Strength, 16–17, 18, 19
Strength training, 19–21. *See*
*also* Agility training; Fitness
training; Flexibility training;
Quickness training; Speed
training; Weight training
Stress, 13, 14, 17, 19, 36, 46, 60,
120, 145, 150–52, 168. *See also*
Emotions; Pressure
Stretching, 104, 119–20, 125–26
Substance abuse, 168. *See also*
Illegal drugs; Steroids
Swimming, 17, 37, 63, 80, 119, 148,
153, 170

Tactical abilities, 5–6, 10–11, 23–25,
29, 36–37, 42, 46, 48, 61, 73, 102,
126, 149, 183
Taking Credit (attribution), 85. *See*
*also* Attributions
Taking the Blame (attribution),
85–87. *See also* Attributions
Tapering, 148. *See also* Burnout;
Overtraining; Staleness
T-ball, 160
Tebow, Tim, 172
Technical skills , 5–6, 10–11, 23–25,
28, 36–37, 42, 46, 48, 53, 73, 78,
102, 126, 130, 139, 149

Tennis, 11, 18, 20, 23, 24, 28, 46, 52,
62, 106, 130, 145–47, 157
Thorpe, Ian, 28, 80
Thought-stopping, 79–80, 97,
104–6
Timely goals, 58–59. *See also* Goal
setting
Time management, 151
Title IX, 188
Track and field, 12, 16–17, 104, 115,
116, 126, 130, 143, 148, 165, 168
Training. *See* Agility training;
Fitness training; Quickness
training; Speed training;
Strength training; Weight
training
Tugnutt, Ron, 157

Ultimate goal, 55, 63. *See also* Goal
setting
Uncontrollable factor, 11–15, 60,
105, 106, 180. *See also* Luck
U.S. archery team, 139–40, 142
U.S. men's soccer team, 30, 61–62
U.S. national basketball team, 9
U.S. Olympic Center, 180
U.S. Open (golf), 76
U.S. Open (tennis), 158
U.S. Soccer Federation, 78, 180
U.S. Tennis Association, 130
U.S. women's soccer team, 26–28,
98–99
University of Alabama, 172
University of California at Los
Angeles, 29
University of Connecticut, 20
University of Delaware, 20
University of Florida, 172

University of Illinois, 78
University of Iowa, 7
University of Kentucky, 157
University of Mississippi, 172
University of North Carolina, 71, 149
University of Oklahoma, 172
University of Southern California, 40, 181

Violinists, 1
Visualization, 119, 142; *See also* Imagery; Mental practice
Volleyball: 11, 18–19, 20, 37, 46, 52, 165; beach, 12

Wake Forest University, 9, 167
Warm-up, 103, 119, 121, 125–29, 131; *See also* Pre-performance routine
Webb, Jerome "Spud," 11
Weight, 15, 16–18
Weight training, 16–17, 18–19, 115, 149. *See also* Agility training; Fitness training; Flexibility training; Quickness training; Speed training; Strength training
Williams, Serena, 106
Wimbledon, 158
Women's American Basketball Association, 188
Women's Basketball League, 188
Women's National Basketball Association, 188
Wooden, John, 29, 168
Woods, Tiger, 51–52, 57, 76–77
Work ethic, 30, 57. *See also* Hard work
World Championship for Triathletes, 171
World Cup (soccer), 29, 61–62, 98, 105
Wrestling, 7, 16, 18, 115, 165

Year-round training, 153–54; *See also* Burnout; Overtraining; Staleness

Zone of optimal functioning, 117–22, 125–26. *See also* Energy: management